ISBN 978-1-334-03080-2
PIBN 10661885

This book is a reproduction of an important historical work. Forgotten Books uses
state-of-the-art technology to digitally reconstruct the work, preserving the original format
whilst repairing imperfections present in the aged copy. In rare cases, an imperfection in
the original, such as a blemish or missing page, may be replicated in our edition. We do,
however, repair the vast majority of imperfections successfully; any imperfections that
remain are intentionally left to preserve the state of such historical works.

# 1 MONTH OF
# FREE
# READING

## at
## www.ForgottenBooks.com

By purchasing this book you are eligible for one month membership to ForgottenBooks.com, giving you unlimited access to our entire collection of over 700,000 titles via our web site and mobile apps.

To claim your free month visit: www.forgottenbooks.com/free661885

English
Français
Deutsche
Italiano
Español
Português

# www.forgottenbooks.com

**Mythology** Photography **Fiction**
Fishing Christianity **Art** Cooking
Essays Buddhism Freemasonry
Medicine **Biology** Music **Ancient
Egypt** Evolution Carpentry Physics
Dance Geology **Mathematics** Fitness
Shakespeare **Folklore** Yoga Marketing
**Confidence** Immortality Biographies
Poetry **Psychology** Witchcraft
Electronics Chemistry History **Law**
Accounting **Philosophy** Anthropology
Alchemy Drama Quantum Mechanics
Atheism Sexual Health **Ancient History**
**Entrepreneurship** Languages Sport
Paleontology Needlework Islam
**Metaphysics** Investment Archaeology
Parenting Statistics Criminology
**Motivational**

# LETTERS

### BETWEEN

*Theodosius* and *Constantia.*

*= anghorne,* *johreys*

# THE
# LETTERS

That paſſed between

# THEODOSIUS

### AND

# CONSTANTIA;

#### AFTER

## SHE HAD TAKEN THE VEIL.

---

The Second EDITION, with two additional Letters.

---

' Ce ſera eette paix dont ſa Bonté ſupremé
De ſes varis ſerviteurs remplit la ſainteté ;
Et que poſſede un cœur qui rentrant en ſoi meme
 Enchaſſe tout vanité.  PIERRE CORNEILLE.

 Theſe letters are yet extant in the Nunnery
where Conſtantia reſided, and are often read to the
young Religious, to inſpire them with good Reſolutions, and Sentiments of Virtue.  ADDISON

---

### DUBLIN:
Printed by J. POTTS, at Swift's-Head, in
Dame-ſtreet.  1764.

TO

The RIGHT REVEREND

# WILLIAM,

LORD BISHOP of

# GLOUCESTER.

MY LORD,

TO have let the pen sleep, after your Lordship had pronounced me able to serve the cause of our Divine Master, would have been an act of desertion. Before, I entered the lists only as a voluntier, and possibly,

A 2        like

like moſt other voluntiers, I neither did much good nor much harm. But when you, my Lord, who have given ſuch proofs of your Generalſhip, recommended me to the field, I could no longer ſtay behind, nor, like other military Chaplains, during the heat of the battle, keep my ſtation among the baggage.

But your Lordſhip has been ſo ſuccefsful in your ſpiritual warfare, that you have left little for me to do. You have defended religion with equal happinefs from the uncandid
attacks

attacks of her enemies, and the miftaken kindnefs of her friends. You have put the Wolf to death, and the Nurfe to——No, not to filence, my Lord; for in that cafe fhe muft have been put to death firft at leaft.

But what will your Lordfhip fay to my forces? my forces! that confift of one bare-headed Father, and one defencelefs Nun!

Do you afk, why I have employed Popifh advocates in the caufe? I anfwer, that the circumftances of the parties were

favou-

favourable to my defign, and that THEODOSIUS and CONSTANTIA write not in defence of any particular fect, but in the behalf of Chriftianity. This will fatisfy your Lordfhip.

But party zeal, and political fagacity, perhaps may not acquiefce in fuch an anfwer: I hope, however, I fhall be acquitted of any intention to recommend popery, or arbitrary power; and, then, peace be to party-zeal, and political fagacity!

In truth, to ferve the caufe of rational religion, was my only

aim

aim through the whole of this performance; in which I wish to approve myself, my Lord,

Your Lordship's

most obedient

humble servant,

John Langhorne.

# ADVERTISEMENT.

THE ſtory of Theodoſius and Conſtantia is thus related by the Spectator, No: 164.

Conſtantia was a woman of extraordinary wit and beauty, but very unhappy in a father, who having arrived at great riches by his own induſtry, took delight in nothing but his money.

Theodoſius was the younger ſon of a decayed family; of great parts and learning, improved by a genteel and virtuous education. When he was in the twentieth year of his age he became acquainted with Conſtantia, who had then not paſſed her fifteenth. As he lived but a few miles diſtant from her father's houſe, he had frequent opportunities of ſeeing her; and by the advantages of a good perſon, and a pleaſing converſation, made ſuch an impreſſion in her heart as it was impoſſible for time to efface :

efface : He was himself no lefs fmitten with Conftantia. A long acquaintance made them ftill difcover new beauties in each other, and by degrees raifed in them that mutual paffion which had an influence on their following lives.

It unfortunately happened that, in the midft of this intercourfe of love and friend-fhip between Theodofius and Conftantia, there broke out an irreparable quarrel between their parents, the one valuing him-felf too much upon his birth, and the o-ther upon his poffeffions. The father of Conftantia was fo incenfed at the father of Theodofius, that he contracted an unrea-fonable averfion towards his fon, infomuch that he forbad him his houfe, and charged his daughter upon her duty never to fee him more. In the mean time, to break off all communication between the two lovers, who he knew entertained fecret hopes of fome favourable opportunity that fhould bring them together, he found out a young gentleman of a good fortune and an agree-able perfon, whom he pitched upon as a

A 5                      hufband

huſband for his daughter. He ſoon concerted the affair ſo well that he told Conſtantia it was his deſign to marry her to ſuch a gentleman, and that her wedding ſhould be celebrated on ſuch a day. Conſtantia, who was over-awed by the authority of her father, and unable to object any thing to ſo advantageous a match, received the propoſal with a profound ſilence, which her father commended in her as the moſt decent manner of a virgin's giving her conſent to an overture of that kind. The noiſe of this intended marriage ſoon reached Theodoſius, who after a long tumult of paſſions which naturally riſe in a lover's heart on ſuch an occaſion, writ the following letter to Conſtantia.

‘ The thought of my Conſtantia, which
‘ for ſome years has been my only happi-
‘ neſs, is now become a greater torment to
‘ me than I am able to bear. Muſt I then
‘ live to ſee you another's? The ſtreams,
‘ the fields and meadows, where we have
‘ ſo often talked together, grow painful
‘ to me; life itſelf is become a burthen.
‘ May

' May you long be happy in the world,
' but forget that there was ever such a man
' in it as

'THEODOSIUS.'

This letter was conveyed to Conſtantia that very evening, who fainted at the reading of it; and the next morning ſhe was much more alarmed by two or three meſſengers, that came to her father's houſe one after another to enquire if they had heard any thing of Theodoſius, who, it ſeems, had left his chamber about midnight, and could no where be found. The deep melancholy which had hung upon his mind ſometime before, made them apprehend the worſt that could befall him. Conſtantia, who knew that nothing but the report of her marriage could have driven him to ſuch extremities, was not to be comforted: She now accuſed herſelf for having ſo tamely given an ear to the propoſal of a huſband, and looked upon the new lover as the murderer of Theodoſius: In ſhort, ſhe reſolved to ſuffer the utmoſt effects of her father's diſpleaſure, rather than comply

ply

ply with a marriage which appeared to her
fo full of guilt and horror. The father feeing himfelf entirely rid of Theodofius, and
likely to keep a confiderable portion in his
family, was not very much concerned at the
obftinate refufal of his daughter, and did
not find it very difficult to excufe himfelf
upon that account to his intended fon-inlaw, who had all along regarded this alliance rather as a match of convenience than
of love. Conftantia had now no relief but
in her devotions and exercifes of religion,
to which her afflictions had fo entirely fubjected her mind, that after fome years had
abated the violence of her forrows, and
fettled her thoughts in a kind of tranquillity, fhe refolved to pafs the remainder of
her days in a convent. Her father was not
difpleafed with a refolution which would
fave money in his family, and readily complied with his daughter's intentions. Accordingly in the twenty-fifth year of her
age, while her beauty was yet in all its
height and bloom, he carried her to a
neighbouring city, in order to look out a
fifterhood of nuns among whom to place
his

his daughter. There was in this place a Father of a convent who was very much renowned for his piety and exemplary life; and as it is ufual in the Romifh church for thofe who are under any great affliction, or trouble of mind, to apply themfelves to the moft eminent Confeffors for pardon and confolation, our beautiful votary took the opportunity of confeffing herfelf to this celebrated Father.

We muft now return to Theodofius, who the very morning that the above-mentioned enquiries had been made after him, arrived at a religious houfe in the city where now Conftantia refided; and defiring that fecrefy and concealment of the Fathers of the convent, which is very ufual upon any extraordinary occafion, he made himfelf one of the order, with a private vow never to enquire after Conftantia; whom he looked upon as given away to his rival, upon the day on which, according to common fame, their marriage was to have been folemnized: Having in his youth made a good progrefs in learning, that he might dedicate him-

felf

self more entirely to religion, he entered
into holy orders, and in a few years became
renowned for his sanctity of life, and those
pious sentiments which he inspired into all
who conversed with him. It was this holy
man to whom Constantia had determined
to apply herself in confession, though neither she nor any other, besides the Prior
of the convent, knew any thing of his
name or family. The gay, the amiable
Theodosius had now taken upon him the
name of Father Francis, and was so far
concealed in a long beard, a shaven head,
and a religious habit, that it was impossible to discover the man of the world in the
venerable conventual.

As he was one morning shut up in his
confessional, Constantia kneeling by him,
opened the state of her soul to him; and
after having given him the history of a life
full of innocence, she burst out in tears,
and entered upon that part of her story, in
which he himself had so great a share. My
behaviour, says she, has, I fear, been the
death of a man, who had no other fault
but

but that of loving me too much. Heaven only knows how dear he was to me while he lived, and how bitter the remembrance of him has been to me since his death. She here paufed, and lifted up her eyes that ftreamed with tears towards the Father; who was fo moved with the fenfe of her forrows, that he could only command his voice, which was broke with fighs and fobbings, fo far as to bid her proceed. She followed his directions, and in a flood of tears poured out her heart before him. The Father could not forbear weeping aloud, infomuch that in the agonies of his grief the feat fhook under him. Conftantia, who thought the good man was thus moved by his compaffion towards her, and by the horror of her guilt, proceeded with the utmoft contrition to acquaint him with that vow of virginity in which fhe was going to engage herfelf, as the proper atonement for her fins, and the only facrifice fhe could make to the memory of Theodofius. The Father, who, by this time, had pretty well compofed himfelf, burft out again in tears upon hearing that name, to which he had

been

been fo long difufed, and upon receiving this inftance of an unparalleled fidelity from one who, he thought, had feveral years fince given herfelf up to the poffeffion of another. Amidft the interruptions of his forrow, feeing his penitent overwhelmed with grief, he was only able to bid her from time to time, be comforted—to tell her that her fins were forgiven her—that her guilt was not fo great as fhe apprehended; —that fhe fhould not fuffer herfelf to be afflicted above meafure: After which he recovered himfelf enough to give her the abfolution in form; directing her at the fame time to repair to him again the next day, that he might encourage her in the pious refolution fhe had taken, and give her fuitable exhortations for her behaviour in it. Conftantia retired, and the next morning renewed her applications. Theodofius having manned his foul with proper thoughts and reflections, exerted himfelf on this occafion in the beft manner he could, to animate his penitent in the courfe of life fhe was entering upon, and wear out of her mind thofe groundlefs fears and apprehenfions

ons which had taken poffeffion of it; concluding, with a promife to her, that he
would from time to time continue his admonitions, when fhe fhould have taken upon her the holy veil. The rules of our
refpective orders, fays he, will not permit
that I fhould fee you, but you may affure
yourfelf not only of having a place in my
prayers, " but of receiving fuch frequent
inftructions as I can convey to you by letters." Go on chearfully in the glorious
courfe you have undertaken, and you will
quickly find fuch a peace and fatisfaction in
your mind, which it is not in the power of
the world to give.

Conftantia's heart was fo elevated with
the difcourfe of Father Francis, that the
very next day fhe entered upon her vow.
As foon as the folemnities of her reception
were over, fhe retired, as it is ufual, with
the Abbefs into her own apartment.

The Abbefs had been informed the
night before of all that had paffed between
her noviciate and Father Francis, from
whom

whom she now delivered to her the following letter.

" As the first fruits of those joys and consolations which you may expect from the life you are now engaged in I must acquaint you that Theodosius, whose death sits so heavy upon your thoughts, is still alive; and that the Father to whom you have confessed yourself, was once that Theodosius, whom you so much lament. The love which we have had for one another, will make us more happy in its disappointment, than it could have done in its success. Providence has disposed of us for our advantage, though not according to our wishes. Consider your Theodosius still as dead, but assure yourself of one who will not cease to pray for you in Father

FRANCIS."

Constantia saw that the hand-writing agreed with the contents of the letter: And upon reflecting on the voice, the person perfon, the behaviour, and above all the extreme forrow of the Father during her confeffion, fhe difcovered Theodofius in every particular. After having wept with tears of joy, it is enough, fays fhe, Theodofius is ftill in being; I fhall. live with comfort and die in peace.

"The letters which the Father fent her afterwards are yet extant in the nunnery where fhe refided; and are often read to the young religious to infpire them with good refolutions and fentiments of virtue." It fo happened that after Conftantia had lived about ten years in the cloyfter, a violent fever broke out in the place, which fwept away great multitudes, and among others, Theodofius. Upon his death-bed he fent his benediction in a very moving manner to Conftantia; who at that time was herfelf fo far gone in the fame fatal diftemper, that fhe lay delirious. In the interval which generally precedes death in ficknefs of this nature, the Abbefs finding that the phyficians had given her over, told

told her that Theodofius was juft gone before her, and that he had fent her his benediction in his laft moments. Conftantia received it with pleafure: And now, fays fhe, if I do not afk any thing improper, let me be buried by Theodofius. My vow reaches no farther than the grave. What I afk is I hope no violation of it.——She died foon after, and was interred according to her requeft.

Their tombs are ftill to be feen, with a fhort latin infcription on them to the following purpofe.

Here lie the bodies of Father Francis and Sifter Conftance. They were lovely in their lives, and in their deaths they were not divided.

Such is the ftory of Theodofius and Conftantia, as related by Mr. Addifon; on which I fhall only obferve that there is an interpolation in the letter written by Theodofius upon leaving his father's houfe. The paffage where he fays, " the ftreams, the fields,

fields, the meadows, where we have so often talked together, grow painful to me," is not genuine, which indeed might be evident to thofe who had not feen the original. Such romantic trifling is not the language of a heart in pain.

The following letters are thofe which in the foregoing ftory are faid to be ftill extant in the nunnery where Conftantia refided. By what means, or with what difficulty, I procured thofe letters, which were never before publifhed, it is not neceffary to inform the reader. And I am fenfible that no apology need be made for publifhing them, in a country where the monaftic life is juftly condemned. The great principles of religious obedience are the fame under every communion; and if thefe letters fhall be found to contain any thing that tends to the melioration of the heart, or the enlargement of the mind; if they plead not idly in the defence of religious happinefs; if, when the interefts of futurity are placed in competition with the purfuits purſuits that terminate in the grave, the letters of Theodoſius ſhould throw any thing into the ſcale, I ſhall rejoice that upon this occaſion I have not laboured in vain.

JOHN LANGHORNE,

FEB. 21, 1763.

LET-

# LETTERS

BETWEEN

## *Theodosius* and *Constantia.*

---

## LETTER I.

### THEODOSIUS to CONSTANTIA.

THE efforts which a mind in trouble makes to regain its loft peace, like the glances of the fun that ftruggle through oppofing clouds, are delightful to all beholders. When my Conftantia rofe above that gloom of forrow, which her too apprehenfive heart had thrown around her; when I faw her eye brighten, and her elogant but dejected features affume that beautiful form in which nature had moulded them, I fhould have felt the pleafure of a Chriftian, had I not once been Theodofius.

Amiable mourner! Let us now forget the name which you have fo long remem-

B                                                   bered

bered with anguiſh, and which you could not pronounce without trembling, when you affectingly told Theodoſius that you believed him to be no more. I wept, my Conſtantia, but my concern aroſe not from a ſenſe of your guilt, but of your ſufferings. Thoſe tears, indeed, fell from the eyes of Theodoſius, and in them the Confeſſor had no part. The powers of memory and reflection were, in one moment, preſented with every ſcene of diſtreſs and tenderneſs which our unhappy loves had produced. And when I conſidered myſelf as the unfortunate cauſe of your long, your unmerited ſufferings, I felt, in one painful minute, what Conſtantia had endured for years. Perhaps, too, your unequalled fidelity and unaltered love, while they flattered my heart, brought it back a moment to the world.—But my guardian Spirit whiſpered me that I had made a higher choice, and reminded me that the duties I owed you were thoſe of a ſpiritual director, from whom you were to receive conſolation and inſtruction. But, before I proceed to the further diſcharge of thoſe duties, let me intreat you to forgive me—forgive me, ſuffer-

ing

ing innocence, for being the unhappy, though involuntary, inftrument of your many miferies.——— Five unchearful years! my Conftantia! How has your gentle heart fupported itfelf during that melancholy period? How has it fuftained thofe cruel apprehenfions which, in confeffion, fhook your frame? The reflection of what you muft have endured for me, as it then wrung my foul with anguifh, yet clouds it with forrow, and has power to difturb the ferenity of a mind, which, I truft, hath been vifited by the peace of God.

But I fhould be ftill more difconfolate, were I not well affured that your prefent happinefs will be in proportion to your former fufferings, and that the difficult ways through which you walked, have at laft conveyed you to the manfions of peace.

Such, Conftantia, is the lot of human life. The road to happinefs is feldom ftrewed with flowers, nor perhaps ought it to be fo; as we fhould, in that cafe, be inclined to take our paffage for our port, and,

while

while we enjoyed the manna, we might neglect the promised land.

I am, however, of a different opinion from moft men with regard to the fufferance of moral and natural evils. They derive them from the hand of providence, and charge the confequences of human paffions, follies and vices, upon the divine adminiftration. I remember to have feen a Liturgy for the vifitation of the fick, wherein the minifter was directed to inform the fick perfon that whatever he fuffered, it was the vifitation of God. Would this exhortation have been proper for a perfon who was labouring under difeafes, that were the natural and inevitable effects of intemperance? Can thofe pains which the fufferer has confcioufly and voluntarily brought upon himfelf, be deemed the vifitation of God? With regard to this doctrine, my Conftantia, it is, of confequence that you fhould be rightly informed, becaufe from miftaken apprehenfions of providence proceed almoft all the errors of religious faith. But moft dangerous to ourfelves, and moft

injurious

injurious to the Deity, are thofe opinions
which magnify his defpotifm at the expence
of his benevolence. Hearken not to fuch
opinions, Conftantia: God cannot be the
minifter of evil.

Our fufferings, natural and moral, are
the confequence of that freedom of will
which is the very effence of our moral
powers, and without which we fhould be
mere machines, incapable of all virtue.
There are indeed fome natural evils which
to incur or avoid depends not upon ourfelves, becaufe they come not within the
œconomy of reafon. But of thefe we partake only in common with mankind; and
as in the difpenfation of fome of thefe we
can perceive that providence had wife and
gracious purpofes, fo we may fairly infer
that thofe whofe final caufes we cannot apprehend, have their origin in the fame uni--
verfal Benevolence.

It is, I think, generally underftood, as
a doctrine founded upon revelation, that
there are fuch things as divine inflictions

even.

even in this life. No doubt there may be such, and there may be seasons obvious to the eye of providence, when it is good for us to be afflicted. We may be summoned by calamity from the festive pursuit of pleasure, and though we cannot perceive the hand, the writing may be divine.

But I believe that this interposition of the supreme power is very rare. Nay I will own to you, Constantia, that my faith in this doctrine is, at best, but diabolical; for, while I believe, I tremble. Will God do evil that good may come? Is it necessary? If it be necessary, God may do it.

I will moreover warn you of the evils that may be derived from this doctrine. It may prompt us to vain comparisons and uncharitable constructions: When we behold the calamities of others, we may be inclined to trace the finger of God where it has not been, and when we tacitly refer to our own condition, we may impute our exemption from evil to that integrity whereof we ought not to boast.

Under

Under the mofaical difpenfation prefent inflictions were more vifible, becaufe more neceffary: For, what other reftraint was there upon the moral actions of mankind? When the great fanctions of Chriftianity were fet forth, thofe reftraints became inconfiderable, and were totally abforbed in the interefts of the new fyftem. Old things paffed away; behold! All things became new.

But we are too apt to mix our religion, and to incorporate the divinity of the Old Teftament with that of the New. The law indeed ftill remains in force, becaufe its tendency was everlafting; but when God faw fit to enter into a new covenant with man, the difpenfations of his providence were altered, and made agreeable to it. Thus, though under the old law it might be neceffary for the divine power to chaften whom he loved, yet that meafure could be no longer expedient, when the hopes and fears of mankind were appealed to by the fanctions, of immortality.

It

It is of great importance to you, Conſtantia, to form a right idea of your Creator, and to know in whom you have believed. To affiſt you in this reſpeçt, will
be one of the firſt endeavours of Father

FRANCIS.

# LETTER II.

## CONSTANTIA to THEODOSIUS.

MY forrows for Theodofius are no more: He lives, and Conftantia is happy. If you would not have me remember my fufferings, forget them yourfelf; for nothing now could make the reflection of them painful to me, but their affecting my revered Father.

Gracious Providence! And have I at length found a father? Has heaven granted what nature refufed? She gave me indeed a father; but he forgot the name; or he remembered the name and the authority, but forgot the duties of the alliance. Do I err? Then inftruct me, my holy guide, inftruct me to revere the man who banifhed Theodofius, and imbittered without caufe, the moments of her whom he had brought into being. But I will revere him, for he was kind at laft, and permitted me to retire to this afylum of peace. What-

ever

ever were his motives, I will revere him ;
for have I not here found the only comfort
I was capable of? Am I not sure that Theodosius lives? Without that conviction (I
own my weakness) I should have been unhappy within these holy walls. The exercises of devotion I pursued with equal assi-
duity and attention for years before I entered upon the conventual life; but my
prayers were the heavy sacrifices of sorrow
and contrition. I was alike a stranger to
the serenity of peace and to the alacrity of
hope. It was not in the power of conscious
penitence to set my heart at ease, whenever
the cruel thought presented itself, that my
cowardly acquiescence in the will of a father had been death to the most valuable
and most amiable of men. Pitying heaven
has at length undeceived me, and at once
restored to my eyes those dear lamented fu-
gitives, Theodosius and happiness; both
changed indeed, but both improved by the
change. The pleasure I enjoyed in the
company of the elegant and lively Theodosius, was gay, sprightly, and animated
like himself: With him it departed and
returned;

returned; and my heart was alternately delighted and depreſſed. Very different is the ſatisfaction I now feel. It is ſerene and peaceful like Father Francis. My mind is collected, and my ſpirits are repoſed. No longer agitated with the anxieties and impatience of hopes that terminate here; my eye is fixed on that diſtant, invariable object of happineſs, on which time or chance can have no influence.

Ye holy retreats! Ye venerable ailes! do I owe this peace to you? No, not to you: for methinks I have ſeen in your regions the gloom of diſcontent. Is it not, my pious Father, from a quiet conſcience that I derive this repoſe? I ſhould not, indeed, have felt it before I entered this convent, but I ſhould not then have known that Theodoſius was ſtill in being.

Do not think, however, that I rejoice not in my ſituation. I do rejoice in it: But my joy ariſes, as I apprehend, from a diſburthened mind. The ſudden change from painful apprehenſion to the certainty of con-

firmed

firmed wifhes, was attended with a tranf-
port, the effects of which I ftill feel. But
will not thefe effects laft? Surely they will.
O my friend! what tears of joy have I fhed
over that firft welcome letter, which informed me that Theodofius was ftill alive!

But do I not forget that I am addreffing
myfelf to the venerable Francis? Pardon
me! I had indeed forgot, till on re-perufing
that ever-dear letter, I beheld the holy
name at the bottom. Yes! delightful letter! fweet meffenger of peace! Thou in-
formeft me that I muft confider Theodofius ftill as dead.—Ha! dead, did'ft thou
fay? Theodofius is ftill alive. Didft not
thou fay that too? Equivocating letter!
Begone into my bofom: but prefume not
there to fay that Theodofius is dead.

Heavens! what rambling is this? Whither has my unguided pen betrayed me?
Once more forgive me, my revered Father!

I thank you for the comfort, as well as
for the information which your laft letter
afforded

afforded me. You have placed the Eternal Providence in a light the moſt amiable, and new, at leaſt to me. I had always, hitherto looked upon that power as the inflicter of temporary evils, and conſidered both private and public calamities as his judgments. But you have now made me of a different opinion; and I entirely agree with you, that temporary rewards and puniſhments are ſuperſeded by the ſanctions of the chriſtian religion. Neverthelefs I am ſtill of opinion that God may occaſionally interpoſe, by the infliction of evil, to ſave a wretch who is thoughtleſly or obſtinately haſting to deſtruction; but, with you, I apprehend that ſuch diſpenſations are very rare, and am, for the reaſons you mention, almoſt afraid to believe them.

One thought, however, occurs to me on this occaſion, which I ſhall take the liberty to mention, in conſequence of the invitation you have given me to expreſs my ſentiments without reſerve.

We

We are fo entirely different in our powers and paffions, and the circumftances of fin and temptation are fo extremely various, that though the Almighty might in general leave it to the fanctions of religion alone to influence the actions of men, yet poffibly he might (fo to term it) referve a difcretio-nary power, to bring proper objects by af-flictions to their duty.

But though the creator of the univerfe can in no fenfe be the author of evil, it can-not be doubted, I apprehend, that he may, and frequently does, bring good out of evil. Of this the ftory of Jofeph is, in all its circumftances, a remarkable proof. I cannot fuppofe, neither would you have me believe, that God infpired the brethren of Jofeph with envy, that they might fell him into Egypt, or that, when fold, the wife of Pharaoh was influenced by a fupe-rior power to accufe him falfly; yet, what glorious advantages did the Almighty Pro-vidence bring out of both thefe events!

And

And has he not, for he regards the humbleft of his creatures, has he not for me turned the path of forrow towards the harbour of peace? I will believe it, left I fhould prove ungrateful. Pray for me and inftruct me. Adieu!

CONSTANCE.

## LETTER III.

THEODOSIUS to CONSTANTIA.

GOOD fenfe, Conftantia, makes better comments than learning, and I find that to propofe my opinions to you will be of advantage to myfelf.

But do you not err, my amiable friend, and is there not fome acrimony in your language, when you fpeak of your natural father? It muft not be. The duties of parents and children are indeed reciprocal: But the unnatural parent cannot acquit the child of its duty, any more than the undutiful child can acquit the parent of his natural obligations. Both thefe however are to be underftood as fecondary to the great duties we owe ourfelves. A child ought no more to embrace mifery than vice to oblige a parent, and a parent is under no obligation to forfeit his own happinefs for the gratification of a child. But, under all circumftances, that refpect which is due to a parent ftill fubfifts ; and when

Conftantia

Conſtantia reflects on this, ſhe cannot with-
hold that reſpect. Pity your father, Conſtantia; pray for your father. If the God
of this world hath blinded his eyes, fer-
vently pray for him in the words of Saint
David, " O God, lighten his eyes, that he
ſleep not the ſleep of death." He bears no
uncommon marks of guilt or infamy. His
foible is the love of money; a paſſion which
of all others is the moſt difficult to guard a-
gainſt, becauſe it increaſes by impercepti-
ble degrees; and when it has once got entire poſſeſſion of the heart, I believe that
there is no remedy for it. Many liberal
men have become covetous, but I never
yet knew one covetous man who became
liberal; ſo eaſy is it in every inſtance to
deviate from virtue to vice, and ſo hard in
that particular caſe to riſe from vice to virtue. Let us then conſider your father as
an object of compaſſion, and by no means
forget to offer up our prayers for him. Who
knows whether heaven may not liſten to
the voice of ſupplicating innocence, and be
overcome by the intreaties of filial piety?
would it not throw a new glory around the

brows

brows of Conſtantia, ſhould her father be
reſtored to virtue by her prayers?

You are in the right, Conſtantia, to aſcribe your preſent happineſs to peace of conſcience; for that is the foundation of all moral and religious comfort. Without that
the hallowed walls of a cloyſter would be
hung with horrors, and the gloomy retreats
of a convent would adminiſter melancholy
to the mind. It is that alone which gives
ſerenity to our devotion, and enables us
properly to communicate with God. It is
that which the apoſtle of the Gentiles, in
his ſecond letter to the converts of Corinth
and other parts of Achaia, offered to their
conſideration, to take off that concern and
ſorrow which thy muſt have felt for the
perſecutions which he and the reſt of his
fellow-labourers had undergone in their
travels through Aſia. The confidence of
the conſcious mind, he informs them, in
every painful, every trying calamity, had
ſtill ſupported them. Nay, continues he,
we can even rejoice in our diſtreſſes, and
our

our rejoicing is this, the teftimony of our confcience.

Perhaps there is no paffage in the facred writings which more beautifully and more emphaticallly expreffes this moral fenfe or confcience, than that of the Proverbialift. The fpirit of a man is the candle of the Lord, fearching all the inward parts. Heaven, fays the wife man, has placed its candle within us, whofe rays can pierce the moft fecret receffes. No thought fo complicated but it can trace it to its origin ; no idea fo abftracted which its light cannot difcover. If we fhould fay that the darknefs fhould cover us, that the clouds of night fhould veil us from its ray; behold the darknefs is not darknefs with it, the day and the night with it are both the fame. This attends us thro' every circumftance of life; it accompanies thought thro' all the variety of its excurfions, and marks the fource and the progrefs of action. Confcience fits as judge in the mind, and approves or condemns our defigns and actions, as it fees them juft or unjuft, agreeable
ble

able or contrary to the laws of God and
nature. If we have done well, it teaches
us to rejoice in the reflection; and if evil,
it fails not to punish us with a painful sense
of it. From hence arises the continual happiness of the good man, and the never end-
ing disquiet of the guilty. Hence virtue
is said to be its own reward, from the pleasures of reflection; and hence it is, that
there is no peace to the wicked. Whatever artifice they use to silence conscience,
or escape its reproaches, though sometimes
these may be so far successful as to encourage them to commit greater crimes, yet
the judge will again return to the charge,
and they will find that he has slept only to
wake with double vigour and fury. Some
indeed there are who seem to have quite
banished this inhabitant from their breasts;
and to have extinguished the divine lumi-
nary: who go on in a continual course of
wickedness, and have no fear of God
before their eyes. But if we more strictly
attend to the lives and actions of these men,
we shall find that the noise and triumph
they make in their guilt, proceeds not so
much

much from the fatisfaction it affords them, as from an endeavour, however unfuccefs- ful, to ftifle the dictates of the friend in their breafts; and could we purfue them into the privacy of retirement, I will venture to fay that we fhould find them either affectedly indolent, or painfully difcontented. Hence appears the fuperiority of confci- ence. Hence it appears that there are no arts fufficient to filence it entirely, and that it may therefore be fuppofed to come from that Being, whofe determinations muft have their effect, and whofe power is not to be refifted.

If we fhould enquire into the defign of providence in thus furnifhing us with this filent infpector, we fhould find that in this cafe, as well as in all others, our God has acted from the dictates of infinite goodnefs. Had we been without this ever active cen- for, what would have been the confe- quence? Too apt we are even now to flight the admonitions of it, and fhould we not ftill more eafily have fallen a prey to temp- tation, had there been no internal monitor

to

to inform us that " this fhould not be done." Would not vice have found many more votaries, when no meeting remonftrance checked it, and no painful reflection followed? It is evident then that confcience was ftationed in the human mind by the giver of all good gifts; and that for the aid of virtue and for the fupport of reafon, it came down from the Father of lights. Is not this, Conftantia, our guardian angel, who warns us againft the moft dangerous of all enemies, the enemies of our falvation? By this friendly fpy we are informed of, and even forefee, their attacks; and happy it is for us that we are thus affifted. The infinuations of vice, after all, are too often fuccefsful, and her arts prevail againft the force of conviction. Nor indeed, fhould we confider all the ftratagems fhe makes ufe of, would there be any room to wonder at her fuccefs. Does fhe not affume the characters of pleafure, knowledge, virtue, nay and of religion too; her great patron being confcious that he fhall be moft fuccefsful in his works of darknefs, when he affumes the appearance

of

of an angel of light? Does not the moſt profligate licentiouſneſs call itſelf pleaſure? Does not mole-ſighted infidelity claim the titles of Knowledge and Philoſophy? Has not religion.been aſſerted by blood-thirſty zeal? And has not fanatic hypocriſy like-wiſe aſſumed her banner, and lifted up her voice in the ſtreets? O conſcience! Thou ſacred guardian of rational virtue and reli-gious truth, let looſe thy vengeance upon theſe monſters, theſe peſts of ſociety, and emiſſaries of vice!

Do not you perceive, my Conſtantia, in this diſpenſation of providence, the perfec-tion of wiſdom and goodneſs? There are a thouſand vices, a thouſand enormities which have nothing to fear from any human tri-bunal, but are checked and reſtrained by this mental judge.

That peace which you imputed to a diſ-burthened mind, led me naturally into theſe ſentiments. Will that peace, you aſk, con-tinue? Doubt not that it will. It is that peace which the world cannot give, and which,

which, therefore, the world cannot take away. That happinefs which is derived from a pleafing concurrence of earthly e-vents, will vanifh when Fortune reverts her wheel; the fame chance which reared the brittle fabric of felicity, may demolifh it in a moment; but religious fatisfaction, if rightly founded, cannot be overthrown.

I am well affured, Conftantia, that you will find your happinefs increafed by the repeated exercifes of devotion. It is im-poffible that the intercourfe we have with Infinite Goodnefs fhould not be attended with prefent advantages.

But ever let it be your care, my amiable friend, that your devotion be rational and ferene. Let it not rife upon the wings of paffion, but be offered up with a fubdued and difpaffionate decency. Let your mind be clear and compofed when you addrefs yourfelf to your God, left by any means you fhould fpeak unadvifedly to the Father of wifdom, and offer the facrifice of fools.

Wonder

Wonder not if I tell you that all your paffions fhould not be abforbed in heaven. Rational devotion is not founded in the glowing ardours of human fenfibility; the more it partakes of thefe, the more remote it will be from that fpiritual and intellectual worfhip which is paid to the father of lights by fuperior natures. The adoration of paffion is blind and impulfive; that of reafon is clear and intelligent. By this worfhip the Deity is rationally honoured, by that he is implicitly adored.

For thefe reafons, Conftantia, I would not recommend to you thofe books of flaming devotion, which, while they kindle the heart, confufe the head, and turn fober piety into wild enthufiafm. If the authors of fuch books meant to ferve religion, they were miftaken; for true piety differs as much from fuch enthufiaftic ravings, as the chearful temper of ferene health from the delirious wildnefs of a fever. God is a fpirit, and they that worfhip him muft worfhip him in fpirit and in truth. Whatever is fpiritual is difpaffionate. Such

C

is God himself, and such ought to be the worship we offer him.

Adieu! my Constantia. May God keep you in his protection, and enlighten you by his grace.

FRANCIS.

LET:

## LETTER IV.

### CONSTANTIA to THEODOSIUS.

THEODOSIUS is not dead. The polite Theodofius ftill lives in the venerable Father Francis  When I received your laft favour, my hand trembled, and my heart fhrunk. Every idle, every wild ex- preffion, every effufion of vain imagination and uncorrected paffion, that had dropt from my pen when I laft wrote to you, rofe up and reproached me before your feal was broken. While I read the firft period of your letter I frequently took my eye from the paper, and endeavoured to recol- lect the contents of my own. With fear and apprehenfion I proceeded from line to line; but when I found that you had overlooked many of my foibles, and touch- ed the reft with fo delicate, fo indulgent a hand—O my paternal friend! what floods of tender forrow fell from the eyes of your Conftantia! Surely the kindnefs of thofe whom we revere, and are confcious of

having -

having offended, is more cruel than their severity could be. The heart would oppose itself against severe treatment, and call in pride to its aid: But against the force of kindness there is no shield.

In what an amiable light do you represent that Goodness which brought us into being! Conscience was undoubtedly one of his gracious gifts. That moral inspector whose suggestions so lately gave me pain, is now the principal author of my happiness, and I find that conscience is not more severe as an enemy, than kind as a friend. Was it not this that supported the sufferer of Uzz, and was he not animated by the suffrage of Conscience, when he wished that man might be permitted to plead his cause with God. If I am mistaken, correct me, my guide, my father and my friend!

CONSTANCE.

LET-

# LETTER V.

## THEODOSIUS to CONSTANTIA.

I AM pleafed with your reference to the book of Job, as it gives me an opportunity to tell you with what delight I have always read that beautiful dramatic poem. The divine author of it had facrificed to truth and nature. His character of the pious fufferer, however exalted, is not exaggerated by any unnatural ftrokes. While he is not permitted to fall into impious exclamation againft the decrees of providence, he complains of his diftrefs with the fenfibility of a man to whom wearifome nights were appointed. Hence the afflicted patriarch fometimes alarms us with paffionate wifhes for death, and fometimes awakens our compaffion with affecting fighs for his former happinefs.

In the paffage you have referred to, we are prefented with another turn of mind. " I am fenfible, fays he, of the innocence

C 3                              " of

" of my life.  I have done no wrong, nei-
" ther has any violence been found in my
" hands, and yet my face is deformed with
" weeping; and the fhadow of death frowns
" upon my eye-brows.  Yet thus circum-
" ftanced, and thus innocent, my prayer
" furely may be heard.——Behold, even
" now my witnefs is in heaven, and my
" advocate is in the realms of the higheft.
" My friends continually deride me; but
" my tears plead filently with God.  O that
" a man might plead his caufe with God,
" even as the fon of man pleadeth the caufe
" of his friend."  In another of his fpeeches
there is a paffage much to the fame purpofe.  " O that I knew where I might find
him, that I might come even to his feat, I
would order my caufe before him!"

· There is no doubt, Conftantia, that in
thefe fentiments the Patriarch was animated
by the fuffrage of confcience.  And there
is not a paffage in his whole ftory that is
fraught with more important inftruction:
For it may teach us that, under all the circumftances,

cumſtances of human calamity, our only
refuge is in the eternal providence; and
that our peace muſt be derived from that
approving conſcience which may encourage
us to refer our cauſe to God. From what
other ſource can we, in ſuch circumſtances,
look for happineſs? Dependent beings have
it not to beſtow. Were man in his ſocial
nature a more exalted creature, the diſpenſation of peace would not be in his power.
He could not remove from others thoſe
evils to which he ſhould himſelf be ex-
poſed, nor brighten the proſpects of futurity, whither his influence cannot reach.

Man, as a being circumſcribed in his nature, and ſubject to events which he cannot command, muſt, if left to himſelf, fluc-
tuate in uncertainty, and ſtruggle with diſappointment; he, therefore, that would
hope with confidence, and enjoy with ſecurity, muſt have a reſource which time
and chance cannot affect. This can only be
in that independent Being, in whoſe hands
are the iſſues of life and death.

Shall

Shall we truſt to human power? The ſtrength of man is but as the graſs of the field, and all the goodlineſs thereof as the flower that fadeth. Shall we truſt to human riches? Riches profit not in the day of wrath. Shall we truſt to human wiſdom? Wiſdom herſelf is the daughter of affliction. Shall we truſt to human friendſhip? In the day of adverſity there is no hope in man. Can power preclude the attacks of misfortune? Can riches delight in the hour of mourning? Can wiſdom guard againſt the ſtratagems of chance? Has friendſhip a charm for the languor of ſickneſs? How feeble would theſe ſupports prove, Conſtantia, in the trying hour of adverſity, or in thoſe moments of awful ſuſpence, when we expect that the everlaſting doors of futurity ſhall be thrown open, and we ſhall enter in!

Better founded, my friend, will be the ſupports of that man who refers his cauſe to God, and whoſe conſcience encourages him to rely on the eternal providence. He depends on a power that is ſuperior to all
events;

events; on the riches of divine goodnefs, which can never be exhaufted; on that wifdom which can fee the remoteft confequences of things; and on that friendfhip which no caprice can change. The man of Uzz had the ftrongeft conviction of this truth: For experience had taught him that human greatnefs was lighter than vanity itfelf; that riches did actually make themfelves wings and flee away; that the wifdom of man was little more than that of the wild afs's colt; and that his friendfhip was fcarce in proportion to his wifdom. His three friends, whofe knowledge fhould have directed, and whofe affection fhould have foothed him, he often heard, with reafonable impatience, prefcribing refolutions to which human nature was not equal, endeavouring to deprive him of his greateft fupport, the confcioufnefs of his integrity, and fharpening his pains by mortifying reflections. Then it was that, deftitute of all earthly confolation, he appealed to heaven, and even wifhed that by a perfonal communication with the fupreme Power, he

might

might be permitted to lay his caufe before him.

It is our happinefs, Conftantia, that this appeal of the patriarch is not neceffary for us. The Chriftian covenant, gracious in every difpenfation, has given us an advocate with the Father, who fhall plead our caufe: An advocate who knoweth well the frailties of human nature, and whofe interceffion can never be ineffectual. Let us, my friend, make ourfelves acceptable to him; let us, lay hold of thofe terms of redemption which he has procured for us, and our eternal interefts will be eftablifhed on a fure foundation.

You, my Conftantia, are among thofe that have chofen this good part; you have laboured for the bread of immortality, and have left that which perifheth to the numbers who difquiet themfelves in vain. Let fuch be pitied, my friend, and not defpifed; for fpiritual pride has its origin in fuch contempt, and it is one of the many unchriftian qualities of blind enthufiafm; Nay, you
fhould

should even watch over your pity; for there is a kind of pity that is allied to contempt.

Born with the gentlest heart, and ever accustomed to adore, with the purest piety, the author of your being, your religion is become habitual, and you know not the difficulty with which a heart long devoted to vice must be reformed.

Man, though born with faculties to reach through the depths of time, and powers to flourish through the ages of eternity, seldom looks beyond the present hour, or is affected but by present objects. The immortal soul confined to this mansion of earth, becomes enamoured of her habitation, and in time persuades herself that here she has a delight to dwell. Hence she is solicitous how she may repair the tottering wall, and support the frail fabric——Yet surely this attachment is strange, Constantia; since notwithstanding her solicitude for its preservation, this frame will soon fall, and very soon moulder into its native earth. Yet a
little

little while, and every breaſt that is now
warm with hope, and buſy with deſign,
ſhall drop into the cold and ſenſeleſs grave.
The eye that is reading this page ſhall be
cloſed in darkneſs, and the hand that writes
it ſhall crumble into duſt.

In that hour when the immortal ſpirit
ſhall exchange this tranſient being for the
allotments of eternity—in that awful hour,
Conſtantia, what ſhall ſupport us? Nothing
but the conſciouſneſs of a well conducted
life. That divine confidence in the Father
of nature,—that peace of God which paſſeth
all underſtanding—that ſerene affiance—
that exalted repoſe of ſoul—theſe are the
fruits of a life long reſigned to God, and directed by religion. Yet ſurely theſe are
well worth our tranſient labours: If theſe
are not ſecured, we have lived and we have
toiled in vain, we have given our money
for that which is not bread, and our labour
for that which ſatisfieth not.

Live,

Live, my Conſtantia, ſupported by that gracious power whom you ſerve, ſupported by his providence, and enlightened by his grace.


FRANCIS.

# LETTER VI.

## CONSTANTIA to THEODOSIUS.

WELCOME, fweet peace of confcience! Lovely ftranger! Daughter of religious duty, welcome! How heavy was my heart, how painful my hours in thy abfence! How gloomy and diffatisfied—— with what anxiety and uneafinefs did I arife from the moft comfortable of all duties, the holy facrifice of prayer! The incenfe feemed to rife unacceptably: my prayers were feeble; they were unable to reach the throne of the Almighty, and returned, but not with happinefs, to my own bofom. To the poffeffion of thee, fweet peace, what are riches and honours? What were the wealth of kingdoms, the acquifition of worlds purchafed at thy expence?

O my paternal friend, how forcible is truth, divine truth! With what pleafing conviction did every ray of it, that illumined your laft letter, fhine upon my heart! How

poor

poor did the interefts, the pleafures of this world appear, when compared with the pure, the peaceable wifdom that cometh from above!

Father of lights, ever grant me this wifdom! Let the prayers of my father and my friend co-operate with my own, at thy eternal throne, and procure for me the bleffed influences of thy facred fpirit.

This, my venerable guide, is the fubftance of my daily prayer, which fince I received your inftructions, I have repeated with greater affiduity. I have ever been convinced that the divine concurrence was neceffary to affift us in the difcharge of our duty, as well as to direct us in the knowledge of it; but that emphatical prayer which concludes your letters, " that the " eternal providence would enlighten me " with his grace," has given new force to my convictions.

I will not prefcribe to you the fubject of your letters. I fhall liften with pleafure and
attention

attention to your inftructions, to whatever
point of duty or of doctrine they may be
directed; but allow me to wifh, my revered friend, that on this important doctrine
of grace I may foon receive your valuable
obfervations.   /

Poffibly this divine difpenfation; may be
neceffary in a greater or in a lefs degree than
I fuppofe it to be. I have received different accounts of it from the profeffors of
our holy faith, but L think that all of them
have concluded it to be neceffary for us;
though in what meafure it was neceffary
they have not agreed.

It is generally underftood that this divine
grace is the confequential privilege of chriftianity, purchafed for us by him who died
for our redemption; yet I have fometimes
thought that the author of the book of
Pfalms prayed for this enlightening grace,
in that paffage which you have quoted in
one of your letters, My God, lighten mine
eyes, that I fleep not the fleep of death.

                                    With

With refpect to this opinion, as well as to the neceffity or expedience of divine grace, and the degree in which it is difpenfed, I await your kind inftructions.

Thofe books of flaming devotion, which you have advifed me not to read, I own I have hitherto been too fond of. Particularly fince I entered upon the conventual life, I have been much converfant in fuch books. They were recommended to me by my lady abbefs, who is a good woman; but her devotion feems not to be of that ferene and temperate kind which you defcribe and approve. She is unequal in her religious deportment, being fometimes elevated, but more frequently depreft.

What do I not owe to you, my Father, for procuring me the book of God in a language I underftand? Agreeably to your directions, I make that my principal ftudy, and truft that it is able to make me wife unto falvation.

Never, I hope, in the heart of your Conftantia, fhall that fpiritual pride you mention

mention find a place. I am too fenfible of their unhappy condition who live without God in the world, to look upon them with any other emotions than thofe of pure compaffion. With the heart that is deftitute of religious peace my own has been a fellow fufferer; and fhould I triumph in comparative happinefs or purity——fhould I thence derive any fentiments of contempt for others, the reflection would rather mortify than footh me, fince I fhould appear to defpife in them what I myfelf had been.

The hour of prayer is at hand—I come; daughters of devotion I join you——and now will I once more intreat the Author of life and death long to fpare you for the comfort and fupport of.

CONSTANCE.

LET-

# LETTER VII.

## THEODOSIUS to CONSTANTIA

I INTENDED to make the difpenfation of grace the fubject of a letter, and
I thank you for putting me in a method of
treating it.

Your firft queftion is, Whether this difpenfation was only the confequential privilege of Chriftianity? or whether it was not
alfo the privilege of Judaifm?

The latter part of this propofition you
infer from that poetical petition of the
pfalmift, My God, lighten mine eyes, &c.
——Now, Conftantia, it is obvious enough
to fuppofe that the king of Ifrael might pray
for the illumination of the divine Spirit, as
his fon and fucceffor prayed for wifdom,
though under their fyftem there was no
promife of the ordinary difpenfations of
grace. It would be natural for a people
who were vifited by God, and beheld, on

fo-

fo many occafions, the interpofition of his providence, to apply to him for his affiftance under the conflicts of religious duty. It would be ftill more natural for them who fate in darknefs, to petition for that light, of which fome emanations were communicated in the extraordinary influences of the fpirit, though, agreeably to the fcheme of the eternal and unerring providence, the perfection of it fhould not be difplayed till the fullnefs of time.

This may be fufficient to anfwer your firft queftion, which is rather curious than ufeful.

With refpect to the neceffity or expedience of the divine grace, I have much more to fay. The philofophers of our fyftem who weigh every thing in the fcale of natural obligation, or moral aptitude, exclaim againft this doctrine of grace. If you admit the impulfe of a fuperior agent, where, fay they, is the moral agency of man? Befides, is it agreeable to the fitnefs of things that God fhould prefcribe a law to man,

man, to which his moral powers alone are not adequate? This, continue they, would be to make God an Egyptian taſkmaſter. The moral powers of man muſt be adequate to the duties appointed him, and the doctrine of grace is therefore ſuperfluous.

At this avenue, which is opened by the chriſtian philoſopher, in ruſhes the philoſopher of nature. He takes up the argument where the other laid it down—You have very rightly obſerved, Sir, ſays he, that God would be an Egyptian taſkmaſter, if he gave us a law that we were unable to live up to: Such I inſiſt upon it, is the law that is ſaid to be from him——From him therefore it cannot be.

Thus, Conſtantia, you ſee the conſequence of philoſophizing in religion.—Give up one redoubt to the enemy, and he turns our batteries againſt us. To both theſe ungracious opponents I ſhall give a ſhort anſwer. To the chriſtian ſophiſt I ſay, that the powers of man may be inadequate to the law of religion, though its origin was

from

from God; and to the philosopher of nature I answer, that the law of religion may be from God, though the powers of man are inadequate to it. The same argument will prove both these points.

A perfect law might be given to imperfect beings without any impropriety: It might be given to make them exert to the utmost the powers of their nature, and strain to higher degrees of virtue for the high prize of their calling——it might be intended to encourage an useful emulation, by making still greater degrees of excellence attainable;——it might be designed to prevent indifference and independence, which man would naturally have suffered to grow upon him, when secure, by his own power, of attaining to moral perfection, and of discharging every duty enjoined him. A dependence on the Almighty for assistance in the conduct of life is productive of many advantages. It prevents that pride and carelesness which are too often the effect of security and independence. It opens an intercourse with the Deity by prayer; which,

though

though the moſt delightful part of religious duty, would become unneceſſary the moment that the aid of the divine grace ſhould be found to be ſo.

From theſe co-operating cauſes, Conſtantia, you ſee how expedient is the diſpenſation of grace. How neceſſary it is for us in our preſent ſtate, we need not make appeals to reaſon, but to experience.

To be ignorant of the ſacred truths of religion, and to be deſtitute of the communicable influences of God's holy Spirit, has been always conſidered by good men as the moſt deplorable condition of human wretchedneſs. Hence we find it repreſented in the ſacred writings by the terrible images of darkneſs, of death. Thoſe, ſays the prophet, that ſate in darkneſs have ſeen a great light, and they that were in the region and the ſhadow of death, on them hath the light ſhined.—Awake thou that ſleepeſt, and ariſe from the dead, and Chriſt ſhall give thee light.——My God, lighten mine eyes that I ſleep not in death. This was the the petition of that prince, whofe devotion was fo pure and exalted, that the Almighty himfelf bore teftimony to his excellence in pronouncing him a man after his own heart. And could he, the light of Ifrael——could he, diftinguifhed for his knowledge of the then revealed religion— could he, illumined with the fpirit of prophecy, think it neceffary to pray for the enlightening grace of heaven, and fhould not we much more?——we, who cannot like the prophet, boaft any fuperior portion of the divine fpirit,. and who have yet, with him, the fame propenfities to evil.

On us, indeed, the fun of righteoufnefs hath fhined. To us is difplayed a perfect knowledge of thofe faving truths, thofe exalted doctrines, that were then only feen in types and fhadows. It is our happinefs to know the perfect will of God, revealed by his Son, Jefus Chrift. The facred Scriptures contain every thing neceffary to falvation. There, every moral duty is clearly ftated, and every point of faith fufficiently difcovered. To thefe fountains of light and immortality

mortality we may apply, without deception, for that knowledge which leadeth us into all truth.

Bleffed be the gracious author of our falvation! the veil of partition is now taken away; thofe types and figures, which were the fhadowings of good things to come, are removed, and we know what we worfhip.

It is for us then on whom the light hath fhined, to be willing, at leaft, to rejoice in that light——It is for us with unwearied affiduity to ftudy the holy Scriptures, which are able to make us wife unto falvation. Whatever attainments we make in fcience, if we neglect this, the only true wifdom, our knowledge and our induftry are vain. Whatever fkill, whatever prudence we poffefs in the œconomy of this life, if the acquifition has been made by the neglect of this knowledge, it is fkill that darkens, and prudence that deftroys.

The rude notices of natural reafon alone can never be fufficient to direct us in every

part

part of our conduct. Thoſe lights, though uſeful and univerſal, are liable to be obſcured by the blaze of paſſions, to be enfeebled by vice, or miſled by error. The underſtanding may be made ſubſervient to the heart, and employed in the defence of what we wiſh, rather than what we ought to do. The force of truth may be overcome by habit, and, like the heathen ſtatuary, we may fall down before an image of our own framing. It is eſſentially neceſſary therefore that we ſhould have ſome certain rules of action, ſome plain directions laid down for our conduct, which can neither be perverted by ſophiſtry nor miſconſtrued by error.

Such, Conſtantia, is the neceſſity of that external information which has been ordinarily diſpenſed to us by the Spirit of God; which while I have been attending to, I have not loſt ſight of my argument.

The ſame cauſes which concur to make the outward evidences of the Spirit of God ſo neceſſary for our information, render the

internal

internal aids of his grace as neceffary for our direction and fupport in the difcharge of our duty.

To acquire a confummate knowledge of the holy Scriptures is not alone fufficient to conduct us to the land of everlafling life. Thefe are the leading ftars by which we muft direct our courfe, but other means are neceffary to guard us from the tempeft above, and the fhoals below. The ocean of life is treacherous and uncertain. Many latent dangers await the paffenger, and he is frequently in the greateft peril when he thinks himfelf the moft fecure.

Shall I change the fcene, and fuppofe that we have an earthly paffage to the city that is not made with hands? Yet in that cafe, how many circumftances of danger to the traveller does the allegory afford me! A thoufand accidents concur to make us deviate from the narrow way that leadeth to life. We are on one fide threatened by horrible precipices, on another invited by profpects of beauty. Defpair points out to

us

us the length and difficulty of the journey, and wearinefs importunes us to feek the vallies of repofe.

The object, indeed, at which we finally aim, would infinitely counterbalance every inconvenience. And the fufferings of the prefent time will bear no comparifon with the glory that fhall be revealed among us. But objects placed at a diftance, however important, never ftrongly affect us——As in the attraction of bodies, if thofe with which they fympathize be far removed, they will adhere to others more near, to which they have lefs relation.

Some portion of divine grace, fome mea-fure of God's holy Spirit, is indifpenfably neceffary for every Chriftian. Mere human wifdom, though affifted by the knowledge of the divine revelation, will not always be fufficient to fupport us in our duty. How often, with the conviction of truth upon us, are we infenfibly drawn into the ways of error! How often, in the confcioufnefs of determined integrity, are we betrayed into

vice

vice by the ftratagems of temptation! Tho'
we may in general be very fenfible of our
duty, yet we have not at all times the fame
capacity of attention, nor the fame readinefs of apprehenfion to diftinguifh good
from evil. The faculties of the mind, are
fometimes vigorous, and fometimes languid.
The will is frequently retained by idlenefs,
or folicited by defire, without receiving any
inftructions from reafon; and the œconomy
of the foul is oftener in diforder than that
of the body.

In fuch circumftances, Conftantia, have
we not need of fome fuperior aid? Want
we not the directive influences of the Spirit
of wifdom, to keep us in the narrow paths
of duty? Can there be any doubt that the
ordinary difpenfations of grace are neceffary?

But, in what degree, you afk, is this
grace ordinarily difpenfed? To which I
muft beg leave to anfwer, that God giveth
not his Spirit by meafure. It is enough
for us to know what he hath declared, that
his grace is fufficient for us. It muft be

neceffary

neceſſary in a greater or a leſs degree, in proportion to the different tempers, ſituations and circumſtances of mankind. And to the prayers and endeavours of each a ſufficiency thereof will be diſpenſed. To our prayers and endeavours, I ſay, it will be diſpenſed; agreeably to which we are told, that our heavenly Father will give of his holy Spirit to them that aſk it in his Son's name. And while we are informed that it is God who worketh in us, we are commanded to work out our own ſalvation. Thus, Conſtantia, a ſufficiency of the divine grace is promiſed to our prayers—promiſed to co-operate with our endeavours. And it is thus, that the œconomy of grace interferes not with that freedom ot will on which all our merit, as rational creatures, is founded. Our prayers and endeavours are voluntary acts, and we are conſequently as much at liberty to lay hold of the diſpenſation of grace as of redemption, and as much at liberty to rejeƈt it, to reſiſt or to quench the Spirit.

Were

Were not this the case, Conſtantia; were the diſpenſation of grace entirely independent on our own will, the moral agency of man would be ſuperſeded, and the doctrine of rewards and puniſhments would be vain. If, according to the doctrine of fanatics, the grace of God be an impulſive principle, partially beſtowed, and actuating us as mere machines, then the Almighty has taken our ſalvation entirely into his own hands, and rendered moral virtue an empty name.

But this doctrine will on the concluſion be found blaſphemous to God, and injurious to mankind. For if God be the ſole agent of our ſalvation, to him it muſt be owing if any ſoul periſheth: And if moral virtue be vain, the flood-gates of vice may be thrown open, and the world be overwhelmed with the deluge.

But if God be the ſole author of our ſalvation, and if his grace be an impulſive principle, which we cannot reſiſt, then no ſoul ſhall periſh; for we are expreſly told

that

that God is not willing that any should
perish, but that all should come to repentance. If it should be replied that some do
perish, nay that many go on in the broad
way to deftruction——then I anfwer, that
God has not the power to do what he is
willing to do. He is willing that none
fhould perifh, and yet you fay that fome
do perifh, therefore there are fome whom
he has it not in his power to fave. Now
God is all-powerful, confequently he muft
have difpenfed with his power in that refpect by making the falvation of man conditional. If we accept not the mercies of
the gofpel on the terms that are offered to
us, God himself can do no more for us——
God himfelf cannot act inconfiftently
with his own laws. Every attribute of the
fupreme perfection muft be perfect——Juftice and truth are his effential attributes——
his juftice and his truth therefore muft be
perfect.

You fee, my friend, how wretchedly
founded is that fanatical doctrine, which
reprefents the grace of God as an irrefiftible
principle,

principle, acting unconditionally, and impelling men to salvation. You see what dishonour it would bring upon the Deity, what disorder amongst mankind, and how inconsistent it is with the sacred writings.

If therefore the grace of God be a conditional, not an irresistible principle, it will, as I observed before, be dispensed only in a sufficient degree: That is, it will effectually co-operate with our own endeavours in working out our salvation. More than this we have no right to expect from the grace of God. Infinite wisdom will not do what is not necessary to be done. The extraordinary influences of the Spirit are ceased, because they are no longer requisite; therefore though many miracles may be done by the intercession of departed saints, yet I believe none of those saints, such I mean as existed since the apostolic æra, did any miracles when living*.

D 5            St.

---

* This is a very modest degree of faith for the Father of a Convent: The Editor, for his part, believes as much the living as the posthumous miracles of those Saints.

St. Paul himfelf, in his firft epiftle to the converts at Corinth, tells them that the miraculous power of the holy Spirit fhould ceafe, but that charity, which was a moral grace of Chriftians, fhould ftill remain, in confequence of thofe ordinary difpenfations of the Spirit, that fhould continue with the church.

Whatever, therefore, appears to exceed thefe ordinary influences of grace, the raving flights of enthufiafm, and the rage of fanatic zeal; the fudden impulfes of devotional rapture, and the wild reveries of Tartuffian dreamers; all thefe are the fruits of infane imagination, and cannot proceed from that pure and peaceable Spirit which cometh from the father of lights.

The office of that Spirit is to inform the mind with a right fenfe of its duty, and to animate and encourage it in the difcharge of it. In this light it is properly called by our Redeemer that Comforter which fhould lead us into all truth, and teach us all things.

How

How much are thefe offices mifreprefent-
ed by the followers of Calvin, and by en-
thufrafts of every denomination! What vifionary communications, what fuggeftions of
fick fancy have thofe delirious dreamers
imputed to the Spirit of wifdom! as if
God would render vain that faculty of reafon which characterizes man by his own
image, and as if the enlightening Spirit of
grace would rather obfcure than illumine
the underftanding, thefe unthinking men
have charged upon the operations of that
Spirit the moft extravagant effects of wild
infanity. Under the influence of imaginary
calls fome have preached, and fome have
prophefied. The mechanic has forfaken
his awl, and his wife her diftaff, and with
heads full of glorious vifions, together they
have iffued into the ftreets and highways to
publifh the everlafting gofpel.

It will always be difficult for devout ignorance to diftinguifh between the fuggeftions of imagination, and the influences of
the divine Spirit. Unaccuftomed to abftracted thinking, or even to draw conclu-
fions

fions from the moft fimple propofitions, the
ignorant are unable to form any judgment
or that mode of infpiration, which fhould
be moft confiftent with the wifdom of providence. They confider not that it muft
be more agreeable to infinite knowledge to
invigorate the nobler faculty of reafon, and
to bring the paffions into fubjection, than
by inflaming them to weaken that faculty,
and by fo doing to put darknefs for light.
Hence all the waking dreams of blind enthufiafm are cherifhed and refpected as the
offspring of grace; and the miftaken vifionary afcribes to the author of reafon, fuch
impulfes and communications as could only
exift in a mind where reafon was impotent.

But the delufions of innocent enthufiafm
would hardly deferve attention, were they
not fometimes productive of confequences
that rendered that enthufiafm no longer
innocent. From the belief of divine impulfes the flames of perfecution have been
lighted, and the altars of fuperftition have
been adorned; the fanguinous have been
prompted to indulge their natural thirft of
blood,

blood, and the gloomy have forsaken the
society of human creatures, and inhabited
caves and cells in solitary sanctity. This
species of religious retirement I have ever
condemned; but my objections do not affect the conventual life, for there is great
difference between retiring to a cave in some
unfrequented desart, and entering into a religious society *. Many more than these
have been the effects of mistaken impulses.
The history of the church in every period
abounds with them.

Yet how easy is it, upon reflection, to
guard against these delusions! What is the
end of divine grace? It is only to aid us in
the knowledge and in the discharge of our
duty. Therefore whatever impulse hath
other tendency than these, it cannot be of
God—because it is not agreeable to his wisdom,

---

* There is indeed, as Father Francis observes, a difference between these two sorts of retirement; but, in
the Editor's opinion, the difference lies only in the
mode; for they are equally repugnant to the determinations of providence, which has made the whole
moral duty of man to consist in the social capacity of
serving his fellow-creatures.

dom, to do what is fuperfluous. A fufficiency of his grace is what alone he hath promifed us, and what alone it is confiftent with infinite wifdom to give. Will the Father of lights amufe his creatures with dreams and reveries? Will he fport with their paffions, deprefs and elevate, inflame and diftract them? Will he not rather affift fuch as call upon him faithfully, to bring thofe paffions into fubjection; and to confirm in its proper empire the nobler principle of reafon? Is not fuch the mode of operation that the all-wife Creator would affign to his affifting Spirit? The wifdom that cometh from above, we are told, is pure and peaceable: Such wifdom is congenial with our reafon, which is a clear and fteady principle; and, therefore, it muft act in concurrence with that principle, at leaft its effects cannot be repugnant to its conceptions.

Thus, Conftantia, by the information of the revealed word, and by the ufe of that reafon which God has given us that we may be able to underftand his will, we learn the nature of fuch difpenfations as his wifdom

dom hath thought proper to communicate to us.

I have extended my obfervations on this fubject further than you defired, or might expect, becaufe the doctrine of grace is an important fubject, and the right underftanding of it may not only preferve us from many abfurdities and indecencies in religious duty, but from many dangerous errors both in practice and belief.——When once the heart gives itfelf up to blind fanaticifm, we cannot tell to what attempts it may be feduced, or where the influences of unreftrained, and (what will almoft always be the confequence) of mifdirected paffions may lead us.——When the imagination triumphs over reafon, the œconomy of the mind is deftroyed; and confufion, with infanity in her rear, approaches, and ufurps the empire of the foul.

May every miniftring fpirit of heaven guard the peace of my Conftantia! May her piety be uniformly rational and calm! May the incenfe of her devotion rife from

the

the altar of reason, the voluntary facrifice of gratitude! May fhe ever know whom fhe worfhips, and remember that an intellectual Being requireth an intellectual adoration! In every act of worfhip, and in every point of duty, may fhe be conftantly fupported and directed by the pure and peaceable Spirit of truth! By that Spirit may fhe be enlightened to difcern thofe finer relations that exift between the Creator and the creature, undiftinguifhed by the eye of human intelligence, and learn from thence not only what is due, but what is acceptable to God. Under every circumftance of life may fhe be happy in eafe, or contented in refignation; and when the fhort thread of life is fpun, when fhe enters upon the inheritance of immortality, may fhe receive the fullnefs of thofe bleffings which Infinite Benevolence has in referve for thofe that honour him.

FRANCIS.

LET-

## LETTER VIII.

### CONSTANTIA to THEODOSIUS.

HOW beautiful does the religion of Christians appear, when beheld with the eye of reason! How amiable the benevolent author of it! Surely, my revered friend, there is a secret delight in the investigation of divine truths, and the discovery of them affords the greatest of pleasures. Your most obliging letter on the subject of grace gave you, I presume, no less satisfaction in the writing, than it afforded me in the perusal; and I think I can discern, in the more animated passages of that letter, those pleasing sensations you felt when the light of religious truth shone the clearest to your eye. If I am not mistaken in this, and if your pleasure in writing that letter, were equal to that which I found in reading it, you have had a better reward than my poor thanks can give you.

You have justified the scheme of providence in the dispensation of grace against every

every objection that has been or can be brought againſt it. You have placed in a clear light the benevolent purpoſes of the Father of mercies in that diſpenſation, who has made man dependent on him for the aſſiſtance of his divine Spirit, only becauſe he has a delight to give it, and becauſe it muſt be the happineſs and comfort of his creatures to receive it. It plainly appears from your account of it, that the œconomy of grace interferes not with that freedom of will on which all moral goodneſs muſt be founded, and without which we could neither be capable of virtue nor vice, neither intitled to rewards, nor liable to puniſhment. It appears that the moral agency of man may be exerciſed in the application of the divine grace, and that he is at liberty either to apply or to reject it.

With reſpect to the degree in which it is diſpenſed, you have, no doubt, rightly obſerved, that as God will not do what is unneceſſary, no more than a ſufficiency of it will be granted to our prayers: And as to the mode of its operation, it is ſurely con-

fiſtent

fiftent with the wifdom that gave us reafon for our direction, to render by his grace the efforts of that reafon effectual, in fubjecting the paffions, and reducing them to the obedience of his holy laws. By a rational worfhip, you have obferved, in a former letter, that God is moft honoured; when, from a due and difpaffionate confideration of his benevolent works, we come, from a principle of gratitude, to offer him a reafonable facrifice. This facrifice would indeed be no longer reafonable, were we irrefiftibly impelled to offer it by the influences of a fuperior agency: We fhould then be the inftruments of a worfhip paid to God, but we fhould not be the worfhippers; and with what delight fhould the eternal wifdom look upon our facrifice, when confcious that it proceeded not from a voluntary difcharge of duty, but was the inevitable confequence of his own agency? With what propriety could he fay, Well done, thou good and faithful fervant, when he himfelf had been the agent, and the fervant no more than a machine in his hands? To fuppofe then

that

that the divine grace is an irrefiftible principle, muft be to charge God foolifhly; and whatever reverence I have heretofore paid to thofe mifdeeming enthufiafts who hold this doctrine, I muft now retract it, and fhall, for the future, rather pity them as miftaken, than refpect them as infpired.

But I will own to you, my paternal friend, that I fhould not fo eafily have become the difciple of reafon, had you made that faculty a dictator on its own authority; but when you only make it inftrumental in the application of truths revealed, as that is, undoubtedly, the purpofe for which it was given us, I cannot but agree with you in every conclufion you have made.

How fhall I thank you for the repeated inftances of your care and kindnefs, for thofe ardent wifhes that glow in the laft page of your letter——thofe prayers for your Conftantia's happinefs and fafety ? O may they be heard at the throne of everlafting:

lafting mercy! and rife not unaccompanied with thofe daily offerings which fhe delights in making for the prefervation of her friend. Adieu!

CONSTANCE.

## LETTER IX.

THEODOSIUS to CONSTANTIA.

AS you were not difpleafed with my account of the difpenfation of grace, I will now give you my thoughts on a duty, to the due difcharge of which that difpenfation is promifed. I have obferved before, that, were the grace of God an unconditional and irrefiftible principle, our prayers would be vain. Had the almighty providence formed an irreverfible decree with refpect to our falvation, or were he totally uninfluenced by any thing that we fhould do in order to obtain the aid of his facred Spirit, our acts of devotion would be as abfurd as every other act of duty would be fuperfluous. Yet there are many, Conftantia, who hold this doctrine: Becaufe the Chriftian covenant is called the covenant of grace, they annihilate the moral agency of man, and reprefent him as entirely paffive in the accomplifhment of his falvation. I have fufficiently expofed the errors of this

unfcriptural

unfcriptural doctrine, and fhall therefore proceed to confider prayer as one of the means of grace.

Our Saviour himfelf, who died for our fins, and rofe again for our juftification, (that is for our deliverance from eternal death; for the word juftification, in the facred writings, generally fignifies deliverance, and in that fenfe I underftand it in this paffage) our Saviour himfelf, I fay, whofe merits with the Father were the primary means of procuring us this grace, expreſsly convinceth us that it is to be obtained by prayer. For in the firft place, this was the method by which he propofed to obtain it for us——I will pray to the Father, fays he, and he will fend you another Comforter, who fhall abide with you always; and in the next place, he affures his difciples that his heavenly Father will give his holy Spirit to them that afk it. The paffage is exprefs to the purpofe. " I fay unto you, afk and it fhall be given you, feek and you fhall find, knock and it fhall be opened unto you. For every one that afketh

afketh receiveth, and he that feeketh findeth, and to him that knocketh it fhall be opened. Which of you, being a father, if his fon fhall afk bread, will give him a ftone? Or if a fifh, will he for a fifh give him a ferpent? Nay and if he fhould afk an egg, will he give him a fcorpion? If ye, then, being evil, know how to give good gifts to your children, how much rather fhall your Father, who is in heaven, give the holy Spirit to them that afk him?" The pains that the divine reafoner hath taken to convince his difciples upon this point of faith, are very remarkable. He firft commands or rather exhorts them to offer their prayers to God; then for their encouragement he affures them that fuch prayers are heard and granted; and afterwards for their conviction, he infers an undeniable conclufion from a parity of reafon. Thus there remains no doubt, that as the mediation of Chrift is the primary, fo prayer is the fecondary means of grace.

In what words, then, and with what fpirit fhall we pray?——Wherewithal fhall we we come before the Lord, and humble ourſelves before the high God? Is not, it may be aſked, that form of prayer which our Saviour taught his diſciples, comprehenſive of all our wants, and ſufficient for the Chriſtian church in all ages? Should this queſtion be put, I would anſwer in the negative. The prayer which our Saviour taught his diſciples was a temporary form. The redemption of mankind was not then accompliſhed. The means of grace were not effectuated. The Saviour of the world was not aſcended into heaven, and till that aſcenſion, the Comforter, the Spirit of truth, was not granted to the church. If I go not away, ſays he, the Comforter will not come unto you; but if I go away, I will ſend him unto you. It is not probable, therefore, that he ſhould teach his diſciples to pray for that grace which was not yet attainable, nor communicated, except in an eſpecial manner. Some cunning interpreters have, indeed, ſuppoſed that the meaning of " thy kingdom come," in the prayer above-mentioned, is metaphorical, and that the influence of grace is thereby

E                    ſignified;

fignified; but I would afk thefe men, whether it be probable that the wife author of our falvation fhould teach his difciples to exprefs fo important a petition by a ftrained metaphor?—Whether he who taught them plainly to fay "give us this day our daily bread," would not, if it had then been proper, have taught them as plainly to fay, "give us the grace of thy holy Spirit," or to have expreffed themfelves in fome other form of words as clear, and as much to the purpofe. Had the words, thy kingdom come, no fignification that was literally obvious, they might as well have been wrefted to one fenfe as to another; but the kingdom of God was an expreffion familiar to the ears of the difciples, and to them it required no comment. They knew that it meant the evangelical kingdom of the Meffiah. In this fenfe that petition ftill retains its original propriety, as the Meffiah's kingdom is not yet complete. Another argument that this form of prayer was temporary and is now infufficient, is this, that the apoftles made ufe of other prayers.—To prove this it is not neceffary

to

to adduce a single inftance, becaufe numbers offer themfelves.

Neither is it neceffary for me to inftruct
you, Conftantia, in what words you fhould
pray for the affiftance of the divine Spirit.
Eloquence is in nowife effential to prayer;
it may be neceffary for the perfuafion of
men, but God fetteth it at naught. Let
us not think that we fhall be heard the
fooner for our much fpeaking, nor yet for
the elegance of our expreffion. If we pray
by a fet form, let the language of it be artlefs and unaffected, and in that refpect re-
femble the finglenefs or fimplicity of heart,
with which we fhould offer it to the all-
knowing Wifdom. I would readily give
you fuch a form as I fpeak of, but the
church alloweth not a private ecclefiaftic
to compofe and communicate a form of
prayer. For you, however, whofe underftanding is clear, and whofe memory is re-
tentive, who digeft your thoughts with
propriety, and exprefs them with eafe,
fcarce any form of private devotion is neceffary.

E 2                          With

With regard to the spirit and manner wherewith we ought to approach the eternal Providence, we cannot be too attentive to so important a circumstance. We should endeavour as much as possible, to be serene and recollected. Before we address that Almighty Being, we should meditate a moment on his sublime perfections, and fill our minds with the idea of his glorious attributes. But rather let us contemplate him in his benevolent, than in his juridical capacity. We ought indeed never to be without the idea of the latter, but the first should always have the leading influence on our minds. Our heavenly Father treateth us not as servants, but as sons; our acts of obedience, therefore, to him should be purely filial. He delights not in the prostration of servile fear, but in the chearful worship of reverential gratitude. Let us not approach him with the cries and lamentations of Moloch's worshippers, nor with the self castigation of the votaries of Baal. Yet, on this as well as on every other occasion, let us remember the vast distance between fallen man and his Creator; let us

consider

confider that our God, though feated on the throne of everlafting mercy, is an offended Being, whofe laws we have broken, and to whofe favour we have forfeited our natural right. Thefe reflections will make us approach him with that humble and dependent fpirit, which muft become a frail and erring creature, in the prefence of its almighty and all-perfect judge.

Let the incenfe we offer him be the pure and undiffembled devotion of the heart. Let us avoid the Pharifaical oftentation of long prayers. Our moral and religious, as well as our natural wants, may be expreffed in few words, that God is not flow to hear. One penitential figh, one humble acknowledgment, will find its way to heaven. One earneft petition for the divine affiftance, one fincere expreffion of gratitude, will be as effectual as a thoufand repetitions. Diffufe and declamatory prayer is a mark of fanaticifm, the bold and extravagant effufion of holy impudence. Shall we think that the Divine Wifdom is to be courted by much fpeaking? Is it neceffary

that

that the sincere of heart should weary Heaven with long importunity? Would not this be to suppose that God is hard to be intreated, or that his ear is obstructed, and cannot hear? How brief is that temporary form of prayer which our Saviour taught his disciples! Does that form contain one superfluous word, or one mere collateral or unimportant thought? Is the imagination indulged in vain descriptions, or are the passions rouzed to eager imprecations? As if the divine author of it had foreseen the idle prolixity of those ranting prayers which should be used in future ages of the church, he has in the above mentioned form been remarkably concise. There is not, perhaps, in any language, an instance of composition where so much is expressed in so few words.

It must be owned, however, that to express our thoughts with brevity and precision, must be the effect of literary skill with us, as it was of divine knowledge with the author of the disciples' prayer. But from the brevity of that prayer we may learn,

learn, what may be of more general use, to say nothing to God that is unneceſſary. If we look into many of our modern forms of prayer, particularly ſuch as have been compoſed by Chriſtians for their private uſe, and afterwards printed for the ſervice of the public, we ſhall find that this precept has been very much-neglected. With a profuſion of ſelf-abaſing expreſſions, partly taken from the ſacred writings, and partly the coinage of their own imaginations, in ſome ſuch ſtrain as the following, they generally, ſet forward.

❧ Hear me, moſt gracious, and moſt merciful Lord God, hear me. Father of heaven and earth, light and darkneſs, day and night, great Creator of all things, hear the meaneſt of thy creatures. Lord, I am a worm, and no man. I am worſe than the vileſt of thy creatures. I am nothing but wounds and bruiſes, and putrifying ſores : From the crown of my head to the ſole of my foot, there is no whole part in me. I have been wicked, Lord, very wicked. Oh the blackneſs of my ſins ! they cry out for vengeance againſt me, &c."

Such

Such is the nature of those ranting, improper and incoherent prayers which are daily offered up in the closets of many pious Christians. As if they would make a merit of their self-abasement, they are loud in complaining of themselves as the worst of creatures. This is a burlesque upon Christian humility. I have known a pious lady, whose life was one continued scene of devotion, daily repeat these humiliating lines, when she offered up her prayers to the Father of truth and wisdom. Our Saviour's approbation of the Publican's prayer affords no argument in favour of these. The Publican was supposed to be really a sinner, not in the ordinary but in the extraordinary sense of the word; yet even he makes no parade of humiliation. He, though a Publican, does not call himself the worst of men, but saith simply, " God be merciful to me a sinner." This was all that he said, and all that it was necessary for him to say.

These over-abasing forms of prayer are not only improper for the Christian who

leads

leads a regular life, but muſt likewiſe be repugnant to his conſcience, and obnoxious to his ſincerity. It is impoſſible that, while he is ſenſible of his good diſpoſition, and endeavours to live according to the divine laws, he ſhould believe himſelf to be the wicked wretch that his prayers repreſent him.

I have yet one objection more to theſe humiliating rants, theſe effuſions of fanaticiſm. They are not only improper for the good man, but unneceſſary for the ſinner—at leaſt on the part of God they are unneceſſary : For, of God can it be ſuppoſed, that he is ignorant of our conduct and muſt learn it from a multitude of ſelf-abaſing words ? Or ſhall we think that he delights in the frequent mention of that wickedneſs, the practice of which offended him ? Or may we believe that he will be prevailed upon by the loudneſs of tautological exclamation ? If theſe things are not to be ſuppoſed, we ſhall conclude that theſe harangues of ſelf-abaſement are unneceſſary with reſpect to God, and that it

E 5          will

will be more proper as well as more modeſt, for the ſinner to uſe the brief acknowledgment of the Publican.

Long and loud confeſſions of ſin before God, are always a mark of a weak underſtanding; nay, I have known ſome eccleſiaſtics ſo extremely injudicious as to recommend this practice in private devotion, and ſo weak as to adviſe us, in our addreſſes to God to mention particularly the ſeveral ſins we have been guilty of. Is not this to ſuppoſe that God is even ſuch a one as ourſelves? Or is it not to conceive yet more meanly of him? When a perſon is diſpoſed to aſk forgiveneſs of thoſe whom he has offended, and to acknowledge his faults, would a generous mind be delighted with the recapitulation of them? Would it not rather be painful to a generous mind? And ſhall we dare to think that man is poſſeſſed of greater generoſity, or more enlarged conceptions, than that infinite Being from whom he derives both? Why then, ye ſelf-abaſing ſinners, will ye weary

God

God with your mistaken prayers? Why
will ye offer to the divine ear what it delighted not to hear? Can ye not be humble without importuning heaven with your
acts of humility? Is not this a species of
eye service?

Let us consider the parable of the prodigal son, which may in some measure be
looked upon as a form of repentance. He
had meditated, we are told, a short speech
of acknowledgment. "Father, I have sinned against heaven, and in thy sight, and
am no longer worthy to be called thy son ;
make me as one of thy hired servants."
This confession he meditated, and this was
as brief, for the circumstances, as the prayer
of the Publican. But what do we find the se-
quel of the story? We find that this short
speech was rendered still shorter, by the
omission of the last clause. The penitent son,
after he had met with such a gracious reception from his father, probably concluded
that such a humiliating overture would give
him pain,—or if he were about to make
it,

it, the father interrupted him, by calling to his servants, and ordering the best robes. Observe, my Constantia, the skill of the sacred parabolist in this place. And the son said unto him, Father, I have sinned against heaven, and in thy sight, and no longer am worthy to be called thy son.—— But the father said unto his servants, bring forth the prime robe, and put it upon him. Is not the omission of the last clause in the premeditated speech, after such a reception, remarkably beautiful? When this is considered, does it appear in the least probable that the father should either expect, or take delight in a detail of his son's follies and vices?

As an act of repentance, with respect to God, such a detail cannot be necessary: For what is repentance, but a relinquishment of sins, from a conviction that they have offended the Judge of the world?

I have said more on this circumstance than I at first intended, and possibly more than

than you may think the importance of it required : But let it be remembered, that nothing is unimportant that relates to the worſhip of God, and that he who contributes any thing to rectify that worſhip, labours not idly in the ſervice of religion.

For this reaſon, you will favour me with your attention, while I point out ſome other errors that I have obſerved in forms of devotion. Among theſe are impertinent expreſſions, ſuch as have no immediate relation either to the general or particular purpoſes of prayer; ſuch as are introduced merely for parade, or ſuch as have no other end than to fill the harmony of a period, or to form the ſide of an antitheſis. Of theſe I could produce many inſtances, from almoſt every form of prayer, whether public or private, from profuſe expatiations on the paſt and preſent works of God, and from ſuperfluous details of our conduct towards him; when with careful minuteneſs we inform him of circumſtances which he knows better than ourſelves.

Neither

Neither can I approve of thofe devout rhapfodies, thofe fportings of zeal, that holy dalliance with God, which fwell the morning and evening devotions of many pious Chriftians. Thefe defultory effufions are inconfiftent with that reverence which is due to an Almighty Being.

In fhort: Let us, when we pray, be modeft, humble, calm, and recollected; and let our forms of prayer be chafte, fubdued, concife and pertinent.

When we approach the Almighty, let us not borrow our ideas of him from human charaƈteriftics: Let us remember, that his ways are not our ways, neither are his thoughts our thoughts;—that as much as heaven is higher than the earth, fo much are his ways higher than our ways, and his thoughts than our thoughts. This reflection will at all times teach us a becoming reverence for our glorious Creator; and particularly in our addreffes to him, it will fuggeft to us the impropriety of vain and imper-

impertinent declamation, of the oftentatious effufions of holy impudence, and importunate familiarities of forward zeal.

Adieu! my Conftantia. May you offer up your prayers in an acceptable time!

FRANCIS.

# LETTER X.

## CONSTANTIA to THEODOSIUS.

YOUR letters difpleafe me, my paternal friend, they make me difpleafed with myfelf. Every page is a mirror that reflects fome circumftance of folly or ignorance on my paft conduct. When I compare my opinions and my practice with thofe which you recommend, I am mortified with beholding fome effential difference ——But go on, dear, cruel inftructer, go on to humble the proud heart of your Conftantia——Make her fee in yet many more inftances what a weak, ignorant, fhort-fighted creature fhe is.

But indeed you ought to conquer that vanity, which in former days you contributed to ftrengthen; when too prodigal of compliment, you would over-rate the talents of your Conftantia; and, in the humility of tender affection, would profefs yourfelf her pupil! Be patient, and indulge me——You
make

make me fenfible of my weaknefs: I am
yet a woman, and muft complain ; I will
have my revenge, and convince you of your
errors. Do I not owe much of my pride
and vanity to you ? Did you not in the days
of flattering love cherifh and fupport thofe
unferviceable foibles ? Having no other ambition than to pleafe Theodofius, if he appeared fatisfied, with my accomplifhments,
I thought them fufficient : If he praifed my
talents, I believed them to be great; and
was indifferent about new acquifitions of
knowledge. Thus, my friend, I bring a
heavy charge againft you, and impute to
you, in fome meafure, my pride and ignorance. Thus it is, that while your letters
convince me of the latter, I gratify the firft
by a flattering excufe. Poor Conftantia!
how much of human weaknefs doft thou
yet retain !

You have much to do, my venerable
guide, much to do before you fhall have
rendered your pupil as wife and as good as
fhe ought to be.

What

What means this uneafinefs that hangs upon my heart? Surely your letter, your valuable letter, could not caufe it. And yet I think, I had lefs pleafure from it than from any other that you have written to me. Was it becaufe you have not fo often appealed to me by the endearing name of your Conftantia? To you, my confeffor, my guide, and friend, I can open all my weaknefs. What means this uneafinefs that hangs upon my heart?

CONSTANCE

LET·

## LETTER XI.

### THEODOSIUS to CONSTANTIA.

AMIABLE tendernefs! Dear Conftantia! fet your heart at eafe. Exert your reafon; tax your fortitude; call forth the nobler faculties of your mind, and charge them to affert their empire over the wayward paffions.

While we are in this ftate of being, we muft encounter difficulties, and ftruggle with uneafinefs. The heart will often be diffatisfied we know not why, and reafon will ftand an idle fpectator, as if unconfcious of its power. In fuch cafes it ought to be awakened from its lethargy, and reminded of the tafk to which it is appointed. It fhould be informed of the high office it bears in the œconomy of the foul, and be made acquainted with the infidious vigilance of its enemies.

But while we languifh under the uneafinefs of difcontent, we cannot take a more
effectual

effectual method to recover our peace, than to confider the infignificancy of every paffion that centers, and purfuit that terminates here. Suppofe our earthly aims were directed to their object by the favouring gale of fortune; fuppofe our purfuits fhould be crowned with all the fuccefs that flattering hope affigns them, yet— vain, changeable, and impotent as we are, the fuccefs would not be worth a moment's triumph. While the heart turns upon an earthly axis, like the perifhable ball that it loves, it will be varioufly affected by outward influences. Sometimes it will bear the fruits of gladnefs, and fometimes be the barren defert of melancholy; one while it will be exhilarated by the funfhine of pleafure, and again it will languifh in the gloom of difcontent. The caufe of this is, not only that the human heart is in itfelf changeable and uncertain, deriving its fenfations from conftitutional influences, but that the objects, if they are earthly objects, on which it depends for happinefs, are liable to variation and decay.

Hence

Hence arises the superiority of religious views. When our hopes of happiness are fixed on one certain event; one event which, though remote, cannot be altered by mortal contingencies, the heart has an invariable foundation whereon it may rest. Without this resting place, we should be tossed to and fro with every wind of fortune, the sport of chance, and the dupes of expectation. To this immoveable anchor of the soul religion directs us in the hopes of immortality. We know from the unerring word of divine revelation, that we shall exist in another state of being, after the dissolution of this; and we are confirmed by every benevolent purpose of providence in the belief that our future existence shall be infinitely happy. In this glorious hope the interests of a temporary life are swallowed up and lost. This hope, like the serpent of Moses, devours the mock phantoms which are created by the magic of this world, and at once shews the vanity of every earthly pursuit.

Compared with this prospect, my Constantia, how poor, how barren would every

scene

scene of mortal happiness appear! How despicable at the best—yet how liable to be destroyed by every storm of adversity! For, are we not exposed to a thousand accidents, the most trifling of which may be sufficient to break a scheme of felicity? Let us consider those conditions that are almost universally desired, the dignity of the great, and the affluence of the rich. Are these above the reach of misfortune? Are they exempt from the importunities of care? Greatness is but the object of impertinence and envy, and riches create more wants than they are able to gratify. Should then our wishes lead to these, we should unavoidably be disappointed. The acquisition might for a while sooth our vanity, but we should soon sigh for the ease of obscurity, and envy the content of those whom pride would call our vassals.

If wealth or grandeur then cannot afford us happiness, where shall we seek it? Is it to be found in the cell of the hermit? or does it watch by the taper of solitary learning? Loves it the society of laughing mirth? or or does it affect the penſive pleaſures of meditation ? Is it only genuine in the cordiality of friendſhip, or in the laſting tenderneſs of married love? Alas! my Conſtantia, this train of alternatives will not do. Should we fly from the troubles of ſociety to ſome lonely hermitage, we ſhould ſoon ſigh for the amuſements of the world we had quarrelled with. The ſtrongeſt mind could not long ſupport the burthen of uncommunicated thought, and the firmeſt heart would languiſh in the ſtagnation of melancholy.

Aſk the ſolitary ſcholar, if ever, in his learned reſearches, he beheld the retreat of happineſs—Amuſement is all that he will pretend to—Amuſement! in queſt of which the active powers of the mind are frequently worn out, the underſtanding enervated by the aſſiduity of attention, and the memory overburthened with uneſſential ideas.

Yet, poſſibly, happineſs may mingle with ſociety, and ſwell the acclamations of feſtive mirth. No—the joy that dwells there cannot

not

not be called happiness; for the noise of mirth will vanish with the echo of the evening, and even in laughter the heart is sad. If we are able to distinguish the elegance of conversation, we shall often be disgusted with the arrogance of pride, or the impertinence of folly; and if not, we may be amused indeed with the noise, but can never taste the pleasures of society.

As little reason have we to hope for lasting happiness from the engagements of friendship, or of love. The condition of human life is at best so uncertain, that it is even dangerous to form any connections that are dear. The tenderness of love, my Constantia, opens the heart to many sufferings, to many painful apprehensions for the health and safety of its object, and many uneasy sensations both from real and imaginary causes. It was from this conviction I told you, in the letter wherein I first discovered myself to you, " that the love we have had for one another will make us more happy in its disappointment, than it could have done in its success."

'For .

For want of a better remedy to these
evils, the wisdom of ancient philosophy
teacheth us to bid a brave defiance to the
assaults of pleasure and of pain. This precept it urges with unremitting austerity;
without making any allowance for particular tempers or circumstances; without in-
structing us how to behave to the solicitati-
ons of joy or pleasure; how to defend the
heart from the inroads of sorrow, or to
guard against the unseen stratagems of dis-
tress.

But the religion of a Christian affords a
nobler and a safer refuge. With the exalted
hopes that this presents to us, the sufferings
of the present time are not worthy to be
compared. In those glorious hopes let us
bury every anxious thought, the uneasiness
of discontent, and the solicitude of care.
Let us not sink under our light afflictions,
which are but for a moment. A very few
years, perhaps a few months or days, may
bring us into that state of being, where care
and misery perplex no more. Though we
have now our bed in darkness, and our pil-

low

low on the thorn, yet the time draweth nigh when we shall taste of life without anguish, and enjoy the light without bitterness of soul. The night is far spent, my Constantia, the day is at hand; let us therefore gird up the loins of our mind, and be sober——no longer dissipated or disturbed with the troubles of this world. We are hourly hasting to that scene of existence, where the wicked cease from troubling, and where the weary are at rest; where hope shall no more be pained with disappointment, and where the distresses of time are forgot in the joys of eternity.

FRANCIS.

LET.

## LETTER XII.

### Constantia to Theodosius.

IS it thus that you hope to reform your Conftantia? Do you think that you fhall be able to effect this by letting her foibles pafs uncenfured, and conveying inftruction to her in general terms? Alas! how little do you know of her petulant and capricious heart! It muft be corrected with feverity, and quieted by overbearing reproof.

At prefent, indeed, it is fufficiently depreft. Your obfervations on the folly and vanity of expecting happinefs in this world came to me at a time, when painful experience convinced me of their truth.

After Theodofius was loft to me, I contracted a friendfhip with an amiable and accomplifhed lady, to whom my melancholy and my misfortunes ferved only to endear me the more. Her good fenfe and her compaffion foothed and fupported me

F 2 under

under all my fufferings. She left me not to the attacks of folitary difcontent, but affiduoufly diverted my mind by the efforts of elegant humour, polifhed fenfe, and ingenious obfervation. As if fhe had preferred the company of forrow to every focial amufement, even in that feafon of life when the heart of health and peace is always gay, fhe never forfook me during the laft five unhappy years. She obferved with unwearied vigilance the hour, when melancholy apprehenfion was increafed to the acutenefs of grief. She then followed me into whatever privacy I fought; clafped me to her faithful bofom, and if, under the agonies of terror and anguifh, tears refufed their affiftance, fhe folicited, and obtained them by her infectious tendernefs. When, at laft, I determined to take the veil, and had obtained my father's confent to forfake the world for ever, her affection followed me in that final refolution. She waited only for an approaching opportunity to fettle her worldly affairs, after which fhe intended to have made one of our fifterhood, and to have

passed

paffed the remaining part of her life with
her Conftantia.

Upon this event my heart repofed. I
forefaw in this a fcene of happinefs that
could not be equalled upon earth, and I
flattered myfelf that it would be as lafting as my own life. How many pleafing
hours have I paffed in meditating on the future felicity of our friendfhip! How often,
in the luxury of imagination, have I confidered our united prayers afcending more ac-
ceptably to the throne of everlafting mercy!
What joy did I promife myfelf, what importance in the eye of friendfhip, by communicating to my Sophia all the inftructions I
had received from my Theodofius.

Oh my friend! my father! thefe hopes
are overthrown. Do I live to tell you by
what means? Sophia, my tender, my dear
Sophia is no more. The uneafinefs I expreffed in my laft proceeded probably in
fome meafure from my pre-fentiments of

F 3                          this

this cruel event. I am now very miserable, and in great need of your paternal
advice.

CONSTANCE.

I E T.

## LETTER XIII.

### THEODOSIUS to CONSTANTIA.

AS true friendſhip is one of the greateſt bleſſings of human life, our ſorrow for the loſs of friends is more excuſable than moſt of our complaints. But, though it may be more venial, it is not more reaſonable than any other mode of miſery that has its origin in diſappointment. Did we think our friends immortal? Did we not know, while we held them to our hearts, that we were embracing the property of Death, who would ſooner or later aſſert his claim?

Our reſignation to this as well as to all other evils ought to be confirmed by reflecting on the univerſal agency of providence. The author of the book of Pſalms furniſhes us with excellent doctrine on this ſubject. We have ſcarce any where ſuch

ſtriking-

striking pictures of human misery as in that
book. The royal writer has described in
the strongest colours the distresses and per-
plexities to which, as men, we are subject.
He has descended to the private dissatisfac-
tions of the heart, and recounted many circumstances of accidental calamity. Hence
it is that his writings are of general use.
Of the distresses that are incident to our being though the prospect be gloomy, it is
necessary we should observe it; as he who
must make his way through pitfalls and precipices, would chuse a plan of the road he
was to travel, rather than march blindly
forward without knowledge and without
caution.

But these are not all the instructions
which the Psalmist affords us. We are seldom presented with an afflicting prospect
of life without being directed to the means
of comfort. We are told that, however
great the causes of our affliction may be,
they are subject to the wise directions of a
Being benevolent to man, and that, though
heaviness may endure for a night, joy cometh

meth in the morning. The doctrine of an universal providence, which is the only source of confolation under every fpecies of mifery, is afferted through this whole book with the greateft confidence of certainty.

" Who is like unto the Lord our God, who hath his dwelling fo high, and yet humbleth himfelf to behold the things that are in heaven and earth ?"

" Thou fhalt fhow us wonderful things in thy righteoufnefs, O God of our falvation ! Thou that art the hope of all the ends of the earth, and of them that remain in the broad fea.

" They alfo that dwell in the uttermoft parts of the world fhall attend to thy tokens—Thou that makeft the out-goings of the morning, and the evening to praife thee."

In this belief of the univerfal agency of providence the Pfalmift places the remedy of moral and natural evil.

F 5 " Should

" Should I find trouble and heaviness, I will call upon the name of the Lord. O Lord, I befeech thee, deliver my foul!

" The Lord preferveth the innocent: I was in mifery and he helped me.

" The proud, O Lord, have had me exceedingly in derifion, but I remembered thy everlafting judgments, and received comfort."

The laft fentiment ought to be engraven upon the hearts of all the children of affliction.

Let us remember that God is the fupreme governor of the univerfe; that under his direction is the whole fyftem of nature, by him animated, connected, fupported. Let us confider that the agency of man in this fyftem is only moral. The œconomy of life is committed to him fo far as it may exercife his moral will. But the events of his actions are finally under the determination of the Almighty. Were not he he to direct the natural courfe of this world, even in thofe circumftances of it that are or may be affected by the moral power of man, order could no more be preferved in the univerfe, than it could at firft refult from chance, or be formed by the direction of fallible beings.

This confideration, that the fupreme Power has in his own hands the œconomy of the world, ought to engage our refignation under every circumftance of life : For, fhould we quarrel with the difpenfations of him who gave us being? Should we difpute the regulations of that power, who has provided the means of this day's fubfiftence, and without whofe favour and protection we could no longer exift ? Is not he who made the world beft able to govern it ? Has not he who gave us this being a right to refume it ?

What mean, then, the pangs of difappointment ? What mean the languifhing complaints of forrow ? The tears that flow

for

for buried virtue, and the sighs that mourn
for parted friendship?

But to these questions you will say that
others may be opposed. You will ask if
these emotions ought to be excluded from
the human heart, when they are evidently
the effect of nature? You will enquire
whether the God of nature would plant affections in his creatures, which to stifle
would be a virtue?

To these questions I would reply, that
those affections for the objects of this world,
which we have received with our being,
may be indulged; but under certain limi-
tations. Let us always confider the end
of such affections. Certainly it could not
be to create us misery, when those objects
are no more; for that would be indirectly
to repine at the dispensations of him who
has removed them from us.

The voice of nature will be heard, and
our tears will flow when our dearest connections

nections are broken. In this we only act like men: But when sorrow is long indulged, it becomes criminal; for then we tamely give ourselves up to those passions which it is our duty to restrain, and act in petulant opposition to the decrees of providence.

Human life must have many avenues to sorrow and anxiety, while we are concerned for the welfare of those objects which have engaged our affections, or the success of those schemes on which all our wisdom has been employed. The duty of resignation, therefore, like every other that is enjoined us, is calculated to promote our own happiness. When we remember the everlasting judgments of God, we may reasonably be filled with comfort in all our tribulations.

" It is the Lord; let him do what seem-
" eth unto him good. It is the Lord, the
" Lord God, merciful and gracious, flow
" to anger, abundant in goodness, and in
" truth.

" Why

"Why fhould ye fay unto my foul, that
" fhe fhould flee as a bird unto the hill?
" Behold the Lord, the Lord of Hofts is
" my refuge; the God of Jacob is on my
" right hand."

Under fuch confidence as this, what have
we to fear, and for what fhould we figh?
That misfortunes feem to counteract our
fchemes of happinefs, and that the profpects of hope are clouded by difappointment, we might mourn indeed, were this
the only fcene of our exiftence, and were
our views terminated by our departure from
it. That human knowledge is often inadequate to the purpofes of life, and always
imperfect, would be a melancholy confideration, were it not attended with the profpect
of an exiftence, where knowledge as well as
happinefs fhall flow from the fountain of infinite perfection. By this view we may ob-
viate the pangs of difappointment, when
prudence is defeated by the caprice of fortune, and when the petulance of chance
has made a jeft of fagacity.

This

This reflection might, one should think, be sufficient to set our hearts at ease with respect to temporary misfortunes, but still more powerful will be the motives to resignation, when we confider that the Father of Heaven has not only promifed us a fafe retreat at laft from our afflictions, but to support us under them.

" Thefe things have I faid unto you, " that in me ye might have Peace: in the " world ye fhall have tribulation.

" Are not two fparrows fold for a far- " thing? and one of them falleth not to the " ground without the permiffion of my Fa- " ther who is in heaven. Are not ye of " more value than many fparrows?

That man in the fyftem of nature has a peculiar regard fhewn him, it would be fu- perfluous to obferve. None of us can be fo blind to the bounties we enjoy, nor to the eminent prerogatives by which we are dif- tinguifhed. But I may infer that as the favour of the Almighty is fo evidently feen in in man, his confidence in him, under every circumſtance of life, ought to be in proportion. If he is diſtinguiſhed by the light of reaſon, he ought not ſurely to make that light an inſtrument to cenſure the perfection from which it flows—yet diſcontent is a kind of cenſure on providence.

Alas! my dear Conſtantia, how miſtaken is the man, how much an enemy to his own happineſs, who confides not in the meaſures, nor reſigns to the diſpenſations of his Creator! He robs himſelf at once of that ſovereign remedy of evil, reliance on a ſuperior power. He is involved in calamities without the alleviation of hope, and ſubject to misfortunes without redreſs.

But happy, above all names of happineſs, is he who with grateful humility ſubmits to the determinations of God. The viciſſitudes of fortune cannot diſtreſs him. He is ſecure in the care of Almighty Goodneſs. Nature may ſhrink back from the ſtroke of affliction, but the conflict that is ſupported by hope can neither be long nor painful.

" Why

" Why art thou so full of heaviness, O
" my soul, and why art thou so disquieted
" within me? Trust in God."

The great object of his hope, the perfect
happiness of a future existence, he knows,
cannot be very distant——that he has but
to travel a few days longer till he reach the
mansions of everlasting rest, where the miseries and delusions of mortality shall vanish,
and sorrow and mourning shall flee away.
Adieu, my Constantia! Think of these
things and be happy.

FRANCIS.

# LETTER XIV.

## THEODOSIUS to CONSTANTIA.

WITHOUT waiting any return to my laſt, I once more ſit down to write to you. I would in ſome meaſure imitate that dear and valuable friend you have loſt, whoſe aſſiduous tenderneſs, you ſay, would never leave you to the attacks of ſolitary ſorrow. This was wiſely done when your grief had continued unreaſonably long, but I am always of opinion that under the firſt ſtages of ſorrow the mind ſhould be left to itſelf; and would our common rules permit me to viſit you, I ſhould decline it till the violence of your grief ſubſided.

The objection, however, does not lie with the ſame force againſt writing to you. We can better bear the ſentiments of our friends, when they are not perſonally witneſſes to our weakneſs.

My

My defign at prefent is not to inftruct But to amufe you. I therefore fend you poetry inftead of philofophy, or rather, indeed, philofophy harmonized; for the fentimental part of the following compofition is large and noble.

PSALM

## PSALM CVII.

1. O GIVE thanks unto the Lord, for he is good; for his mercy endureth for ever.

2. Let the redeemed of the Lord say so, whom he hath redeemed out of the hand of the enemy.

3. And gathered them out of the lands, from the east, and from the west, from the north, and from the south.

4. They wandered in the wilderness, in a solitary way; they found no city to dwell in.

5. Hungry and thirsty, their soul fainted in them.

6. Then they cried unto the Lord in their trouble, and he delivered them out of their distresses.

7. And he led them forth by the right way that they might go to a city of habitation.

8. O that men would praise the Lord for his goodness, and for his wonderful works to the children of men.

9. For he satisfieth the longing soul, and filleth the hungry soul with goodness.

10. Such as sit in darkness and in the shadow of death, being bound with affliction and iron.

## Psalm CVII.

YET once more wake the strain of grateful
　　　　praise,
To that eternal Power, whose mercy shines
O'er all his works, immortal! Let them wake
The grateful strain once more, those happier sons,
Whom his hand rescued from the hostile chain
Of old captivity! From climes remote,
From the first openings of the orient day,
From Hesper's silver floodgates, from the star
That shoots its pale rays o'er the shivering north,
From Egypt's tyrant shores, his parent voice
Their scatter'd trains assembled. Long they stray'd
Thro' wild woods unfrequented; long; nor found
City, or safe abode; till nature sunk
With meagre want opprest, and the faint pulse
Of life beat weakly. Then with humble prayer
To Heaven they turn'd repentant, nor unheard.
Eternal Mercy led the wanderers forth
To habitable towns, and safe abodes.

O for the spirit of exalted praise,
To blazon high those acts of power divine,
Those boundless mercies that embrace mankind!
From him our various appetites and powers,
Moral or sensual, meet supply derive.

They, thrice unhappy! o'er whose joyless heads
Grim darkness hovers; they who lonely dwell
In death's unchearful shade, afflicted, bound

In

23. *They that go down to the sea in ships, that do busines in great waters;*

24. *These see the works of the Lord, and his wonders in the deep.*

25. *For he commandeth and raiseth the stormy wind which lifteth up the waves thereof.*

26. *They mount up to the heaven, they go down again to their depths: their soul is melted because of trouble.*

27. *They reel to and fro, and stagger like a drunken man; and are at their wit's end.*

28. *Then they cry unto the Lord in their trouble, and he delivereth them out of their distresses.*

29. *He maketh the storm a calm, so that the waves thereof are still.*

30. *Then are they glad, because they be quiet, so he bringeth them unto their desired haven.*

31. *O that men would praise the Lord for his goodness, and for his wonderful works to the children of men!*

32. *Let them exalt him also in the congregation of the people, and praise him in the assembly of the elders.*

33. *He turneth rivers into a wildernes, and the water-springs into dry ground:*

34. *A fruitful land into barrenness, for the wickedness of them that dwell therein.*

35.

The bold adventurers on the ſtormy breaſt
Of ocean, tenants of the wat'ry world,
Mark in the mighty waſte of ſeas and ſkies,
Magnificence divine.   At his command
The ſwift wind ſweeps the billows ; up they riſe
Infuriate to the vault of heaven, then down
Precipitately ſteep, diſparting, ope
The vaſt abyſs voracious.   Ah ! where then,
Weak mariners, your hopes ? Then the heart faints.
From ſide to ſide they run, they reel, they fall,
Inebriate with confuſion.   Nought remains
But trembling prayer, the laſt appeal to Heaven.
Nor vain the laſt appeal.   Already, ſee !
The rapid ſtorm ſubſides, and the wave ſleeps.
Alert within the merry ſailor's heart
Springs hope ; and ſoon he hails the welcome port.

O for the ſpirit of exalted praiſe,
To blazon high thoſe acts of power divine,
Thoſe boundleſs mercies that embrace mankind !

From the full choir of undiſtinguiſh'd crowds,
From Wiſdom's choſen ſynod, crown'd with years,
To Him for ever flow collective praiſe !

Where in wild ſweetneſs roſe the ſallying ſpring,
Where ſpread the copious river, where diſplay'd
The vale its verdant honours, barren lies
A dry waſte,  mark of Heaven's avenging hand
When ſacred Juſtice ſpoke the doom of guilt.

G                              But

35. *He turneth the wilderneſs into a ſtanding water, and dry ground into water ſprings.*

36. *And there he maketh the hungry to dwell, that they might prepare a city for habitation.*

37. *And ſow the fields, and plant vineyards, which may yield fruits of increaſe.*

38. *He bleſſeth them alſo, ſo that they are multiplied greatly, and ſuffereth not their cattle to decreaſe.*

39. *Again they are miniſhed and brought low through oppreſſion, affliction and ſorrow.*

40. *He poureth contempt upon princes, and cauſeth them to wander in the wilderneſs, where there is no way.*

41. *Yet ſetteth he the poor on high from affliction, and maketh him families like a flock.*

42. *The righteous ſhall ſee it, and rejoice; and all iniquity ſhall ſtop her mouth.*

43. *Who are wiſe, and will obſerve thoſe things, even they ſhall underſtand the loving kindneſs of the Lord.*

But lo! where once the dry waſte barren lay,
There in wild ſweetneſs flows the ſallying ſpring
There ſpreads the copious river, there diſplays
The vale its verdant honours ; hamlets fair,
Rich harveſts, bluſhing vineyards, golden fruits,
And flocks abundant, the long-famiſh'd ſwain
Beholds delighted.   Heaven's peculiar care
Are all affliction's children : When the yoke
Of ſtern oppreſſion ſinks the weary heart,
Periſh the ſtern oppreſſors; low in duſt,
Low lies each princely head ; while guarded ſafe
As flocks repoſing in their evening fold,
The peaſant ſleeps in peace.   O fight of joy
To faithful Piety! of conſcious pain,
And keen conviction, to the heart of guilt!


This, this is Wiſdom's leſſon to explore
The active ſcheme of Providence ; to learn
His love divine ; and, learning, to confide.

There

There is no employment so delightful to a devout mind as this attention to the visible administration of providence. To contemplate the Creator of heaven and earth in the magnificence of his works, enlarges and elevates the soul——lifts it above the impertinence of vulgar cares, and gives it a kind of heavenly pre-existence. To consider the benevolent purposes for which he called forth this variety and multitude of being, that comes under our cognizance, must be a perpetual source of comfort. A rational creature, that is conscious of deriving its existence from a being of infinite goodness and power, cannot properly entertain any prospect but of happiness. By the imperfection of its nature it may fall into temporary evils, but these cannot justly be the subject of complaint, when we reflect that this very imperfection was necessary to a probatory life, and that without it, there could neither have been virtue, nor the rewards of virtue. Every degree of excellence depends upon comparison. Were there no deformity in the world, we should have no distinct ideas of beauty: Were there no possibility of vice, there would be no such thing as virtue; and were life of

man

man exempt from mifery, happinefs would be a term of which he could not know the meaning.

But I wander from my firft defign, which was not to philofophize. Be wife and happy. Adieu!

FRANCIS.

LET-

## LETTER XV.

### CONSTANTIA to THEODOSIUS.

IF I could pronounce my heart to be perfectly at eafe, you would have the only reward you defire for your kind, your paternal care. But fhall I, on the contrary, avow my ingratitude? Shall I own that this obftinate, this petulant heart is not yet at reft? Could it oppofe itfelf to the united efforts of reafon and religion? Would it neither be foothed by harmony, nor filenced by philofophy? Vain, incorrigible heart!

Indeed, my venerable friend, I muft not diffemble with you : I have not yet recovered my former peace. And yet, why? I have the fame confidence in the adminiftration of providence. I believe as much in his goodnefs, as much in his wifdom. I attend, with the fame readinefs, on the duties of religion, and offer up my prayers with the fame affiance. I agree to every conclufion you have drawn either from mo-

ral

ral or religious arguments. I acknowledge
the propriety, the duty of refignation under every circumftance of affliction, and yet
I am afflicted. I fee the abfurdity of grief,
yet I am grieved? What can I do more?
I fubmit entirely to the difpenfations of providence. My will fubmits: I do not wifh
to recall my departed friend to life : But
this fubmiffion does not clear my heart of
forrow. Surely it has fome connections
which are not obedient to the will, and
from which it derives involuntary pleafure
or pain. Is not this true? We experience
it in all inftances of affection : We are fenfible of attachments we cannot account for;
and as thofe attachments are facilitated or
interrupted, we are happy or miferable independently of reafon or the will. If thefe
obfervations are founded upon truth and nature, I hope I fhall ftand excufed both before you, and at a higher tribunal, for thofe
tears that have fallen over the grave of my
Sophia.

Think not that I implicitly give myfelf
up to the dominion of Sorrow. I have

been

been too well acquainted with her not to know by what means her influence is increafed or abated. I do not deepen the gloom of melancholy by folitary reflection; I feek the fociety of the fifterhood, and endeavour to enter into their amufements, as well as to join their devotions. In thofe hours when I muft neceffarily be alone, if the uneafinefs of my heart hinders the approach of fleep, I have recourfe to my books; till at laft the wearinefs of attention prevails over the force of forrow, and procures me that reft, which the latter would have prevented.

In the courfe of this reading I have met with many things on which I wanted to confult you, but moft of them have efcaped me. Some of thefe, however, I remember. In a book of divinity, which, I fuppofe, muft have been written by one of the herefy of Calvin, the author afferts that " the Almighty has appointed a day of grace " to every man, beyond which there can be " no remiffion of fin *." I muft own I was

startled

* Many of our modern Fanatics, Methodifts, &c. hold this doctrine.

ſtartled by this aſſertion, as it ſeemed to me
to be very conſequential. The following, I
think were ſome of the texts on which he
founded this belief.

" Seek ye the Lord, while he may be
" found; call ye upon him, while he is
" near.

" Oh, that thou hadſt known, even thou,
" in this thy day, the things that belong
" unto thy peace! But now they are hid
" from thine eyes.

" Again, he limiteth a day, ſaying, To-
" day, if ye will hear his voice, harden not
" your hearts."

In another part of his book, he maintains
that it is impoſſible for thoſe who fall into
ſin, after having once been converted, to
repent, or to be ſaved *. This doctrine
he ſupports by the following paſſage in the
epiſtle to the Hebrews :

" It is impoſſible for thoſe who were once
" enlightened, and have taſted of the hea-

G 5                           " venly

---

* This is another doctrine of Fanaticiſm.

" venly gift, and were made partakers of
" the Holy Ghost, and have tasted the good
" word of God, and the powers of the
" world to come; if they shall fall away,
" to renew them again unto repentance:
" seeing they crucify to themselves the Son
" of God afresh, and put him to open
" shame."

To this passage he adds another, selected
from the same book.

" If we sin willfully after we have re-
" ceived the knowledge of the truth, there
" remaineth no more sacrifice for sins, but
" a certain fearful looking for of judgment,
" and fiery indignation which shall devour
" the adversaries. He that despised Mo-
" ses's law died without mercy, under two
" or three witnesses. Of how much sorer
" punishment, suppose ye, shall he be
" thought worthy, who hath trodden un-
" der foot the Son of God, and hath count-
" ed the blood of the covenant, where-
" with he was sanctified, an unholy thing,
" and hath done despite to the Spirit of
" grace ?"

I must

I muſt own theſe texts appeared to me
to make very ſtrongly for his argument;
and yet if theſe doctrines were generally received, I think, they would open more a-
venues to deſpair; for many Chriſtians, I
fear, muſt have ſinned willfully after repentance and converſion. But, poſſibly, I
do not behold theſe Scriptures in a right
point of view. Let me hope for your kind
inſtructions; and pray for your

CONSTANTIA.

LET:

# LETTER XVI.

## THEODOSIUS to CONSTANTIA.

YOU do well to amuſe yourſelf by books and company; that amuſement will divert your melancholy more effectually than any precepts of philoſphy.

But what ſhall I ſay to your controverſial ſtudies? Shall I praiſe you for wearying your eyes over the pages of Calviniſtic dreamers?——for honouring with your attention the groundleſs doctrines of narrow-ſighted fanatics; who either from want of knowledge or of candour, or more probably from want of both, have ſeized a limb of a text, and without attending either to the writer's deſign, or to the analogy of his reaſoning, have founded upon the mere letter, doctrines that diſhonour their God?

Such and ſo founded, are thoſe you have mentioned.

That God hath appointed a certain period in the life of man, beyond which he will not extend his grace to him, is a doctrine which is so far from having any foundation either in reason or revelation, that it is repugnant to the first, and totally unsupported by the latter.

The texts which your author has produced in support of his opinion, have no manner of connection with it.

" Seek ye the Lord, while he may be " found; call ye upon him, while he is near.

The whole chapter from which this passage is taken, refers to the time of the Messiah's first appearance. The prophet breaks out into raptures upon the view of that glorious æra; and apostrophizes to the people that should then be born, exhorting them not to lose the happy opportunity of making an interest with the Redeemer while he was personally present with them.

" O that thou hadst known, even thou " in this thy day, the things that belong " unto

" unto thy peace! but now they are hid
" from thine eyes."

This is Chrift's apoftrophe to Jerufalem,
when he foretold its approaching deftruction. But what, in the name of the feven
wonders, has this to do with the univerfal
difpenfation of grace? The words are particularly applicable to the occafion on which
they were fpoken, and to the object where-
unto they were addreffed. " Unhappy
" city! I wifh thou kneweft, in this thy
" day, while thou art yet undemolifhed,
" or while I am prefent with thee, the
" things that belong unto thy peace, thy
" everlafting peace, the mercies of redemp-
" tion; but now they are hid from thine
" eyes; at this time thou perceiveft them
" not."

Or poffibly thy peace may fignify, thy
temporal peace, and prefervation from thine
enemies, which interpretation the following verfe feems to favour. " But now they
are hid from thine eyes. Becaufe the days
will come upon thee, when thine enemies,"

mies," &c. I incline to this ſenſe; but whether this or the other be the true one, is quite immaterial to the œconomy of grace.

Let us now conſider the laſt Scripture which your author has adduced in favour of his doctrine.

" Again he limiteth a day, ſaying, To-
" day, if ye will hear his voice."

The author of the epiſtle to the He-
brews, in the chapter from whence this paſſage is taken, endeavours to prove the certainty of that final reſt which ſtill re-
mained to the people of God. Thus he forms his argument; ' That there is a reſt
' for the people of God into which they
' have not yet entered, appears from that
' prophetic pſalm of David, which alludes
' to the time of Chriſt's appearance upon
' earth. The prophet, referring to that
' time, faith, To-day if ye will hear his
' voice. You ſee he is determined as to
' the point of time; he limiteth or ſetteth
' apart

' apart a day: Wherefore from this paſſage
' it is apparent, that for you, Hebrews, for
' for you the deſcendants of thoſe who pro-
' voked God in the wilderneſs, and were
' not permitted to enter into his reſt, a final
' reſt ſtill remains, to which you are invited.'

Thus it is, my Conſtantia, that the diſciples of ignorance, folly and fanaticiſm, by
disjointing and miſconſtruing the Scriptures,
contrive their abſurd doctrines; which are
always as much repugnant to reaſon, as they
are unſupported by revelation. For inſtance, the tenet above-mentioned. Is it
conſiſtent with the juſtice or the goodneſs
of God, who has appointed to man a life of
probation, to limit the advantages, which
in his mercy, he has vouchſafed to him, to
a ſhorter term than his life? While he
leaves him ſtill to contend with the enemies
of his ſalvation, will he deprive him of his
principal ſupport, the aid of his grace?——
his grace, which he has promiſed to thoſe
that aſk it, without exception, and without
limitation?

I have

I have done with the firft tenet of your author; let us now fee whether the fecond be
better founded.

It is impoffible, he maintains, for thofe,
who fall into fin, after having once been
converted, to repent or to be faved. This
opinion he fupports by two paffages from
the epiftle to the Hebrews. Without making any remarks on the infallibility of that
epiftle as a rule of faith, without taking notice of the difficulty and the late day of its
admiffion among the canonical books, I fhall
fhew you that your author has made the
paffages he has felected from that book
prove too much. What the writer of the
epiftle means by falling away, in the firft
paffage, and by finning willfully in the laft,
is the denial of the faith they had profeffed,
and openly apoftatizing from it. This is
clear from the conclufion of both the paffages. Thofe who fall away are faid to crucify to themfelves the Son of God afrefh,
and to put him to open fhame. And he
who finneth willfully is reprefented to have
trodden under foot the Son of God, to have

counted

counted the blood of the covenant, wherewith he was fanctified, an unholy thing, and
to have done defpite to the Spirit of grace.

From hence it appears that for a down-
right apoftate there is no hope of repentance or remiffion of fins. But your author
has not confined this terrible denunciation
to open apoftacy. According to him, none
who have fallen into fin after converfion are
capable of being renewed by repentance,
or faved by the redemption of Chrift. This
doctrine is equally unfcriptural, and unrea-
fonable.

Should man, circumftanced as he is, be
expofed by frailty to final punifhment, or
reduced by accidentally falling into vice, to
irretrievable ruin, he might either turn
from the race that is fet before him in hope-
lefs defpondence, or vainly contend with
danger and difgrace. The pilgrimage of
human life is infinitely troublefome and per-
plext. Dangers there are and difficulties
which all muft encounter, which can neither
be eluded by vigilance, nor annihilated
by contempt.

A juft

A juſt man, ſays the author of the book of Proverbs, falleth ſeven times, and riſeth again. In this place a certain is put for an uncertain number ; ſeven times being among the Jews an indefinitive expreſſion, uſed to ſignify any moderate number.

Our Saviour himſelf being aſked how oft a brother ſhould offend and be entitled to forgiveneſs, and whether or not till ſeven times, anſwered, " not until ſeven times, but till ſeventy times ſeven.' From this paſſage we have the utmoſt reaſon to hope that whenever a man ſhall effectually repent, the divine goodneſs will be ready to forgive him. For if we are commanded to receive into favour an offending brother, however frequently he may have trefpaſſed againſt us, ſhall not our heavenly Father in like manner be ready to receive ſuch as turn unto him ? Shall God recommend ſuch a conduct to man as he ſhould not admit in himſelf? Are we not told that the repentance of a ſinner is unexceptionably ſo acceptable to the Almighty, that the angels in heaven rejoice, and congratulate their ſupreme and

affectionate

affectionate Creator on an event fo agreeable to his gracious mind?

The prodigal in the gofpel returns not to his father till he had finifhed his courfe of riot, which was interrupted by nothing but his power to purfue it. He returns not till compelled by neceffity, and therefore his repentance was not a voluntary virtue: But, behold, his father meets him while yet a great way off, and precludes his apologies by the moft endearing reception. We have not, indeed, any account of a relapfe in the accepted prodigal; but we are told that before the execution of his repentance, he faid unto himfelf, 'How many hired fervants of my father have bread enough, and to fpare, while I perifh with hunger?' Some fuch reflections he muft frequently have made, when reduced to diftrefs, and again probably muft have quitted them from various motives.

We want not, however, this inftance to prove that a finner may be reftored to favour after falling away from his former refolutions

folutions and profeffions of obedience. The
example of Peter is a fufficient proof in this
cafe. To this I fhall add another which,
though not of fcriptural authority, is ref-
pectable, and very much to the prefent
purpofe.

Eufebius tells us, that St. John, during
his miniftration to the weftern churches,
caft his eye upon a young man remarkable for the extent of his knowledge, and the
ingenuoufnefs of his mind. The aged apoftle thought that he had difcovered in him
an ufeful inftrument for the propagation of
chriftianity. Accordingly he took particular pains to convert him, and to inftruct
him in the divine doctrines of his great
Mafter. That he might be ftill better acquainted with the fyftem of Chriftianity, at
his departure, he recommended him to the
care of a pious old father, who had fome
authority in the infant church. The youth
continued a while in the duties of his new
profeffion, and attended with care to the
lectures of his venerable tutor. But his
former affociates, when they found themfelves

felves deferted by him, were grieved at
the fuccefs of the apoftle, and exerted
their utmoft efforts to regain fo ufeful and
fo entertaining a companion. They fuc-
ceeded in their attempts, andthe father was
forfaken. The Apoftle after fome time
returned to thofe parts, and " where," faid
he, with impatience, to his aged friend,
" where, my fellow-labourer, is my favourite youth?" " Alas," replied the good old
man, with tears in his eyes, " he is fallen,
irrecoverably fallen: He has forfaken the
fociety of the Saints, and is now the leader
of a gang of robbers in the neighbouring
mountains." Upon hearing this unex-
pected and unpleafing account, the Apoftle
forgot his fufferings and his years, and
haftened to the place of rendezvous, where,
being feized by fome of the band, he defired to fpeak with their Captain. The
Captain being told that a ftrange pilgrim
afked to be admitted to him, ordered him
to be brought before him. But when he
beheld the venerable apoftle, his hopes of
amufement were changed into fhame and
confufion, and the hardy leader of a
band

band of robbers trembled before a poor un-armed old man. He quitted once more the society of wickedness, and lived and died in the service of his Redeemer.

From, hence it is evident, that a relapfe after repentance or converfion, was not looked upon by the primitive Chriftians, nor yet by the apoftles themfelves, as any means of excluding the future mercies of God.

An utter apoftacy, an entire defertion of the faith we have profeffed, and a con-temptuous rejection of the grace we have received, may, according to the author of the epiftle to the Hebrews, render us in-capable of repentance, and utterly difqualify us for the future mercies of God. But fins inferior to thefe will not reduce us to the fame dreadful circumftances. Our Crea-tor knoweth whereof we are made, he re-membereth that we are but clay; and though we may fall, yet we fhall not be caft away, fince he upholdeth us with his hand.

H God

God preserve you, my amiable friend!
—preserve and direct you through the uncertain paths of this world, till you arrive
at the realms of everlasting rest; till your
innocent, your happy spirit shall quit,
without a sigh, the tender frame that confines it, and rise conducted by some smiling
Angel, to the blessed society of good men
made perfect!

Adieu!

FRANCIS.

LET-

# LETTER XVII.

## CONSTANTIA to THEODOSIUS.

THE everlasting doors of futurity are thrown open——The race of life is almost run, and this, probably, is the last time that your Constantia will have the happiness of pouring out her heart to you. ——I am seized with the first symptoms of that pestilential fever, which has been so universally fatal, that it brings with it almost the certainty of death. Now, therefore, before my faculties are overcome by the disease, I devote to you one hour more of a life in which you have had so great a share.

In a situation like this it is natural to look back, and to take a view of the country through which we have travelled, before we lose sight of it for ever. The ways through which I have walked, though in many circumstances peculiar, and unlike the allotment of others, have yet, like

others,

others, been various, and different in the different periods of the journey. Before my prefent illnefs I drew up a fhort view of my life, part of which I will now tranfcribe, that with you it may ferve as an apology for my conduct when I fhall be no more.

*An Apology for the Life of Sifter* CONSTANCE, *written by herfelf, and addreffed to Father* FRANCIS.

You know how early I loft the beft and moft affectionate of mothers. That was a misfortune which, though then only bewailed with tears which had no meaning, left behind it a cloud that overfhadowed the reft of my life. Had my infant years been trained by her, I fhould have acquired the habits of virtue from the influence of example. The want of this was much to be lamented, for there is a happy contagion in the power of living excellence, which, while we admire, we neceffarily imitate. Thofe virtues which we draw from precept or fpeculation are feldom more than fpeculative,

ative, but thofe which we derive infenfibly from the imitation of exemplary characters become lafting and habitual. But, befides the lofs of a happy and an excellent pattern of every female virtue, I was deprived at the fame time of thofe maternal cares, thofe tender affiduities that watch over the young mind, accelerate the progrefs of reafon, and fupply the want of experience by precept. Of thefe advantages I was wholly deftitute, for my father, inattentive to every thing but the acquifition of wealth, thought but little of the improvement of his daughter; or, if he thought of it at all, concluded that fhe would neceffarily improve in proportion to the advancement of her fortune.——Accordingly I was abandoned to the common forms of female education, without thofe private attentions, thofe exemplary influences, which are of infinitely greater importance than all general inftructions.

Thus unapprehenfive and uninformed, in the firft thoughtlefs advances from childhood to maturity, is it to be wondered that

H 3                                    the

the amiable and accomplished Theodofus
fhould find an eafy admittance to a heart
where every paffion was awake, all un-
guarded, and none reftrained.

But the feverity of wifdom itfelf (prudence, you have told me is but the ape of
wifdom) could have had few objections a-
gainft the paffion that I entertained. For
did it not receive a fanction from the object? What did I admire in Theodofius?
Was it a fymmetry of features? Was it
not the mouth that fpoke like the oracles
of wifdom, and the eye that darted through
the depths of nature? While his knowledge enlightened, his fenfibility charmed
me; and while at once he thought my
heart and my mind to expand, is it to be
wondered that he made room for himfelf?
The powers of genius have an irrefiftible
charm for tafte; and while Theodofius was
forming the mind of Conftantia, he was
cherifhing a plant which, like the gourd of
Jonah, as foon as it fprung up, would
ftretch its arms to embrace him.

When

When this intercourse of growing tenderness was at an end, when the obstinacy of ridiculous pride divided the families of Theodosius and Constantia, what did I not feel from the apprehension of being separated from the man I loved? Pride, however, came in to my aid; I shed a few angry tears, and commanded my heart to be at ease.——But, alas! I soon found that Theodosius was dearer to me than I imagined—yet even, with this conviction, by the united influences of pride, and fear, and shame, my natural attachments to him were overborne; and, without consulting either my happiness or my inclination, I had the infatuation to acquiesce with that proposal of my father which banished Theodosius from publick society.

This was the most culpable circumstance of my life—a fault which indeed brought its punishment along with it, and for which the miseries of one period, and the penitence of another, have, I hope, made an adequate atonement.

The years that paſſed between that e-
vent and my admiſſion into this holy retreat were miſerably worn away between
the languor of melancholy, and the acute-
neſs of grief—yet that plaintive and unre-
ſign'd ſtate of mind was not, I truſt, accompanied with any great degree of guilt, ſince it
was not at the diſpenſations of providence
that I murmured, but at the ſuppoſed con-
ſequences of my own folly. That I refu-
ſed with reſolute indignation the man, to
whom, before, I had been ſo weak as not
to deny my hand, was not enough to make
ſatisfaction to my own heart. While I conſidered Theodoſius as dead, and myſelf as
in ſome meaſure the cauſe of his death, between the grief of affection, and the inqui-
etude of conſcience, I was at length reduced to the moſt pitiable ſtate both of body
and mind ; the one emaciated with ſorrow
and watching, and the faculties of the other
almoſt ſunk in ſtupefaction.

Great diſtreſſes are the ſpectres of the
mind, and, as it is fabled of the ghoſts of
ſelf-murdered bodies, they hover o'er the
ſcene

fcene where their object is entombed. Bufinefs and amufement, fociety and folitude
were alike impreffed with the image of
Theodofius——The painful idea purfued
me through every avocation, nor could I
find a retreat from it in the breaft of friendfhip——The fympathifing heart of my Sophia added new foftnefs to my own, and
the tendernefs of her friendfhip made me
feel more fenfibly the lofs of Theodofius.

At laft that dear lamented friend, with
fome few more that pitied and regarded me,
applied to my father for his permiffion that
I might retire into a convent. Their generofity procured me what the voice of nature and the tears of duty had folicited in
vain, and by the irrefiftible offer of dif-
charging the fees of my admiffion, they
prevailed on the father of Conftantia that
fhe might be permitted to take the veil.

Since I entered upon the conventual life,
my conduct has been too well known to
you, if not to need an apology, at leaft not
to be enlarged upon here. But after thofe
afpi-

aspirations of gratitude that rise to heaven, after those truly grateful sentiments which I must ever entertain for those beneficent friends who procured my establishment in this place——what words shall I find expressive of that gratitude which is due to Father Francis?——that tender, that affectionate father, who has nursed my mind with those paternal assiduities, which were somewhat above the most perfect nature of man, which could only flow from a heart, where human sensibility was exalted and refined by the immortal graces, and where God himself elevated and expanded that philanthropy which he loves.

To the ever venerable Father Francis I owe the greatest moral blessings that are attainable in this world, peace of conscience, and rectitude of reason. For the recovery of the first, indeed, little more was necessary than the certainty that Theodosius was alive and happy; but the consolations of the father added to the presence of the friend, and replaced that quiet in my heart to which it had been so long a stranger. Those

Those consolations, however, were not more soothing, than the lessons that attended them were instructive. While from those I derived content and comfort, from these I received the lights of truth and reason, and was taught to look up with an intelligent adoration to that BEING whose essence is GOODNESS and WISDOM. From the consideration of these distinguishing attributes, whenever he shall resume that life which he gave me, I shall resign it into his hands without sorrow, and without fear.

* * * * * * * * *

With difficulty I had written thus far, when the importunity of my disorder obliged me to lay down the pen. I have now resumed it, and will bear it as long as I am able, for while I hold but even an ideal conversation with you, the sense of pain is suspended. Other than bodily pain I have none. The presumption with which my apology concluded, I find, was not vain. I am perfectly indifferent to the approach of death, and agreeably to the kind wish

with

with which you once * concluded a letter,
I truſt that " my ſpirit ſhall quit, without
a ſigh, the frame that confines it."

To you, my deareſt friend, my moſt venerable father, loved by every dear, and
reſpected by every ſacred name, to you,
under the gracious appointments of providence, I owe this happy ſerenity.  By giving me proper ideas of the author of nature,
and the obligations of his creatures, you
have taught me to look on death as one of
his beſt gifts, and on all beyond it without
any apprehenſion.

Behold here the reward of your pious labours! Behold with pleaſure the reſignation
of a mind that you ſtrengthened, of a heart
that you armed againſt yourſelf.

" My heart was grieved, and it went
" even through my reins.

" So

* This laſt letter of Conſtantia and the anſwer of
Theodoſius ſeem to have been written ſome years after the preceding letters.

" So foolifh was I and ignorant, even as
" it were an irrational creature before thee.

" Neverthelefs I am always by thee,
" for thou haft holden me by my right
" hand.

" Thou fhalt guide me with thy coun-
" fel, and after that receive me in glory.

" Whom fhall I have in heaven but
" thee, for there is none upon earth that I
" defire in comparifon of thee?

" My flefh, and my heart faileth, but
" God is the ftrength of my heart, and my
" portion for ever!

And now, O deareft, and moft revered
of men, farewell!——Whether we fhall
meet again in any future allotment of being, is amongft the fecret counfels of Providence.—I truft we fhall.—'Till then indulge one tender farewel from your Conftantia!——Accept one pious, one grateful adieu from

I                    CONSTANCE.

LETTER

# LETTER XVIII.

## THEODOSIUS to CONSTANTIA.

LET not my Conſtantia be alarmed when ſhe ſees that this letter is written by another hand.—Let not that fortitude with which ſhe has ſo greatly ſupported her own ſufferings be diſſolved in weakneſs for her friend, nor that noble tranquillity, with which ſhe beholds the approach of death, be diſturbed when ſhe is told that this hand is on Theodoſius. I doubt not that the eternal Providence, who, in his wiſdom, interwove the intereſts and the paſſions of our lives, has, in his goodneſs, determined that they ſhall cloſe together. If this be one of his gracious diſpenſations, I receive it not only with ſubmiſſion, but with gratitude.—What more could I deſire of the divine Beneficence than that, delivered from this priſon of earth, I might accompany the ſpirit of my Conſtantia to the regions of everlaſting happineſs, to ſome more perfect allotment

lotment in the fcale of being, where the
immortal faculties fhall be refined from
human frailty; and where the powers of
the foul fhall be expanded by a nearer approach to that perfection, from which
they are derived. Animated with hopes,
and fupported by fentiments like thefe,
let us wait without fear the approach of
death, and receive him gladly, becaufe he
cometh as a friend.—Indulge, my Conftantia, the pleafing hope that our fouls will
know each other in their future appointment.—The pure paffions of love and
friendfhip, founded upon, and fupported
by efteem, may laft beyond the grave,
becaufe they have their exiftence in the
foul.—And will not that Being, whofe effence is love, fupport and cherifh thofe connections which are agreeable to his commands, and thofe fentiments which are
congenial with his own divine nature?
Will he, who commanded us, to love one
another, extinguifh in the grave thofe virtuous paffions, which, when living, it was
our duty to cultivate? It is not improbable
that our happinefs in heaven may, in fome

measure,

meafure, confift in the harmonious intercourfe of a perfect fociety ; for I have no
idea of a folitary happinefs even in the regions of perfection. Moreover, from wha
little accounts we find of the angelic ftate
in the facred writings, we fee that the
ideas of affociation and intercourfe are always annexed to them. If then it is not
to be doubted that in our future ftate we
fhall affociate with fome order of beings,
can any thing be more probable than that
we fhould mix with thofe kindred and congenial fpirits, who like ourfelves have had
their appointments on earth, whether in different times and places, or the fame ? if in the
fame which is ftill probable, and if the iden-
tity of our fpiritual natures cannot be deftroyed, why fhould not the characteriftics of
the foul be known in heaven as well as upon
earth ? I am willing to believe, at leaft, that
the eternal Goodnefs will permit this future
knowledge ; and though we know too little of the ftate of fpirits to conceive the
mode of their future communication, yet
this we know, that it is in the power of
God

God to permit what we wifh for, and I truft that, in his kindnefs, he will permit it.

Then, O my Conftantia! for that ftate of exalted friendfhip, where the fears and frailties of mortality fhall be known no more!—For that happy. intercourfe of fpiritual pleafures, which fhall be no longer fubject to the influences of chance or time ; which fhall neither be oppreffed by languor, or difturbed by anxiety! Compared with that ineffable complacency, that fublime delight which even the hope alone of thefe things infpires, what are the fufferings, however peculiar, that we have hitherto endured ?—Were there, indeed, no future ftate of being to commence after this, who would not wifh to be thus agreeably deceived? Who would not wifh to triumph over thofe gloomy apprehenfions, which the thought of annihilation muft neceffarily create, in a being to whom nature has given the love of exiftence ?

But

But if the foretaste of future happiness be so great ;—if, when only contemplated through the imperfect medium of human imagination, it is capable of inspiring such exalted delight, how inconceivably great must the real and perfect enjoyment be ! Let us here, my Constantia, indulge the utmost stretch of fancy—whatever an Almighty, and all-beneficent Being can give, and whatever our glorified faculties can receive, let us suppose our own. He that giveth not of his spirit by measure, he that openeth his hand, and shutteth it not again——shall not he freely give us all things?

When I consider the wisdom and benevolence of that Almighty Being, through whose kindness I have hitherto been supported in life, like my Constantia, I can walk without trembling through the dark valley of the shadow of death. And whence, but from the same consideration, could your tender and apprehensive heart derive that more than manly firmness which

which is vifible in your letter? That information which you fo kindly afcribe to my inftructions, you have drawn from your own experience of the wifdom and the goodnefs of Providence; to whom your gratitude is due for the rectitude of reafon, as well as for every other blefling you enjoy.

I will now no longer withhold your mind from the meditation of that glorious Being, whofe more vifible favours we fhall fhortly obtain. Indeed, my faculties are already too much confufed for regular thinking, and death, I find, makes hafty paces towards me—Accept my laft blefling.

" Blefs, O God! O Father of Nature,
" blefs my Conftantia! fupport her gentle
" fpirit under the conflict of death! and
" lead and conduct her by the light of
" thy countenance to thy everlafting
reft!"

And

And now—Oh! now—farewell, my Conftantia!——my Conftance! my fifter! my friend! by every dear, and every holy name——farewell! I have converfed with you till the laft moment——But——but we fhall meet again.

ADIEU!

F I N I S.

# THE

# CORRESPONDENCE

## O F

## Theodosius and Constantia,

From their first acquaintance to the departure of
THEODOSIUS.

Now first published from the original Manuscripts.

By the EDITOR of the
LETTERS that passed between
THEODOSIUS and CONSTANTIA
after SHE had taken the VEIL.

*Enfans de l' Oisiveté !*      CHAULIEU.

DUBLIN:

Printed for P. WILSON, S. COTTER, E. WATTS,
W. SLEATER, J. POTTS, J. WILLIAMS, and
J. SHEPPARD. M,DCC,LXV.

---

## T O

## GEORGE COLMAN, Efq;

TO live beneath the golden ftar of love,
  With happier fancy, paffions more refin'd;
Each foftening charm of tendernefs to prove,
  And all the finer movements of the mind.———

FROM gifts like thefe, fay what the boafted gain
  Of thofe who exquifitely feel or know ?
———The fkill from pleafure to extract it's pain,
  And open all the avenues of woe.

YET fhall we, COLMAN, at thefe gifts repine ?———
  Implore cold apathy to fteel the heart ?
Would you that fenfibility refign ?
  And with thofe powers of genius would you part ?

AH no ! my friend ; nor deem the verfe divine,
  That weaknefs wrote in Petrarch's gentle ftrain !
When once he own'd at love's unfavouring fhrine
  " A thoufand pleafures were not worth one pain."

THE dreams of fancy foothe the penfive heat
  For fancy's urn can new delights difpenfe :
The powers of genius purer joys impart ;
  For genius brightens all the fprings of fenfe.

O CHARM of every mufe-ennobled mind,
   Far, far abové the groveling crowd to rife !————
Leave the low train of trifling cares behind,
   Affert it's birthright and affect the fkies !

O RIGHT divine the pride of power to fcorn ;
   On fortune's little vanity look down !
With nobler gifts, to fairer honours born,
   Than fear, or folly fancies in a crown !

As far each boon that nature's hand beftows
   The worthlefs glare of fortune's train exceeds,
As yon fair orb, whofe beam eternal glows,
   Outfhines the tranfient meteor that it feeds.

To nature, COLMAN, let thy incenfe rife,
   For, much-indebted, much haft thou to pay ;
For tafte refin'd, for wit correctly wife,
   And keen difcernment's foul-pervading ray.

To catch the manners from the various face,
   To paint the nice diverfities of mind,
The living lines of character to trace,
   She gave thee powers, and fhe the tafk affign'd.

O LAST-LEFT hope of the forfaken ftage !
   The mufe of humour's fole furviving friend !
Shall COLMAN reft, in this *refining* age
   When wit alone, and elegance can mend ?

SEIZE, feize the pen ! the facred hour departs !
   Nor, led by kindnefs, longer lend thine ear ;
The tender tale of two ingenuous hearts
   Would rob thee of a moment and a tear.

J. LANGHORNE.

LONDON,
Nov. 10, 1764.

ADVER-

# ADVERTISEMENT.

AFTER the diftinguifhed favour and attention fo generoufly fhewn by the public, to *the Letters that paffed between Theodofius and Conftantia after fhe had taken the veil*, no apology, perhaps, will be thought neceffary for thefe that follow, or if any fhould be required, the Editor would gladly reft it on motives of gratitude to that Public, by whofe favour he has been fo much obliged.——If the above-mentioned volume of letters might be efteemed a *Free-will-offering*, he is rather defirous that this may be confidered as a *Sacrifice of Thankf-giving.* To fome readers, poffibly, the letters already publifhed may appear more interefting, by others the prefent may be thought more entertaining; and (fuch is the infinite variety of tafte and fentiment) there is no doubt that both thefe opinions will be reverfed. However, with refpect to the monaftic correfpondence, it muft be allowed to have this fuperiority, that it turns, for the moft part, on religious fub-jects; yet the letters that follow, dwelling chiefly on moral philofophy and the œco-nomy of life, muft be allowed to be ufe-ful in the next degree; as they have, in general, fome tendency to promote the hap-

pinefs.

pineſs of human nature, to the improvement of the heart, or the enlargement of the mind: Had they conſiſted only in a rhapſodical intercourſe of amorous profeſſions, the Editor would never have permitted them to ſee the light, from a perſuaſion that books of entertainment, without either moral or intellectual utility, are mere time-traps, whoſe end is only to defraud us of thoſe moments which will never return.

As this volume may, poſſibly, fall into the hands of ſome who are yet unacquainted with the ſtory of Theodoſius and Conſtantia, it is thought neceſſary to print it here as related by the Spectator No. 164.

" Constantia was a woman of extraordinary wit and beauty; but very unhappy in a father, who having arrived at great riches by his own induſtry, took delight in nothing but his money.

Theodosius was the younger ſon of a decayed family; of great parts and learning, improved by a genteel and virtuous education. When he was in the twentieth year of his age he became acquainted with Conſtantia, who had not then paſſed her fifteenth. As he lived but a few miles diſtant from her father's houſe, he had frequent opportunities of ſeeing her; and by the advantages of a good perſon, and a pleaſing converſation, made ſuch an impreſſion on her heart as it was impoſſible for time to efface :

efface : He was himfelf no. lefs fmitten with Conftantia. A LONG ACQUAINTANCE made them ftill difcover new beauties in each other, and by degrees raifed in them that mutual paffion which had an influence on their following lives.

IT unfortunately happened that, in the midft of this intercourfe of love and friend-fhip between Theodofius and Conftantia, there broke out an irreparable quarrel be-tween their parents, the one valuing himfelf too much upon his birth, and the other up-on his poffeffions. The father of Conftan-tia was fo incenfed at the father of Theo-dofius, that he contracted an unreafonable averfion towards his fon, infomuch that he forbad him his houfe, and charged his daughter upon her duty never to fee him more. In the mean time, to break off all communication between the two lovers, who he knew entertained fecret hopes of fome favourable opportunity that fhould bring them together, he found out a young gentleman of a good fortune and an agree-able perfon, whom he pitched upon as a hufband for his daughter. He foon con-certed the affair fo well, that he told Con-ftantia it was his defign to marry her to fuch a gentleman, and that her wedding fhould be celebrated on fuch a day. Conftantia, who was over-awed by the authority of her father, and unable to object any thing to

ſo advantageous a match, received the propoſal with a profound ſilence, which her father commended in her as the moſt decent
manner of a virgin's giving her conſent to
an overture of that kind. The noiſe of this
intended marriage ſoon reached Theodoſius,
who after a long tumult of paſſions which
naturally riſe in a lover's heart on ſuch an
occaſion, writ the following letter to Conſtantia.

" THE thought cf my Conſtantia,
which for ſome years has been my only happineſs, is now become a greater torment to
me than I am able to bear. Muſt I then
live to ſee you another's ? The ſtreams, the
fields and meadows, where we have ſo often talked together, grow painful to me;
life itſelf is become a burthen. May you
long be happy in the world, but forget that
there was ever ſuch a man in it as

THEODOSIUS.

THIS letter was conveyed to Conſtantia
that very evening, who fainted at the reading of it ; and the next morning ſhe was
much more alarmed by two or three meſſengers, that came to her father's houſe one
after another, to enquire if they had heard
any thing of Theodoſius, who, it ſeems,
had left his chamber about midnight, and
could no where be found. The deep melancholy

lancholy which had hung upon his mind
fometime before, made them apprehend
the worſt that could befall him. Conſtantia, who knew that nothing but the report
of her marriage could have driven him to
ſuch extremities, was not to be comforted:
She now accuſed herſelf of having ſo tamely given an ear to the propoſal of a huſband,
and looked upon the new lover as the murderer of Theodoſius : In ſhort, ſhe reſolved
to ſuffer the utmoſt effects of her father's
diſpleaſure, rather than comply with a marriage which appeared to her ſo full of guilt
and horror. The father ſeeing himſelf entirely rid of Theodoſius, and likely to keep
a conſiderable portion in his family, was
not very much concerned at the obſtinate
refuſal of his daughter, and did not find it
very difficult to excuſe himſelf upon that
account to his intended ſon-in-law, who had
all long regarded this alliance rather as a
match of convenience than of love. Conſtantia had now no relief but in her devotions and exerciſes of religion, to which her
afflictions had ſo entirely ſubjected her
mind, that after ſome years had abated the
violence of her ſorrows, and ſettled her
thoughts in a kind of tranquillity, ſhe reſolved to paſs the remainder of her days in
a convent. Her father was not diſpleaſed
with a reſolution which would ſave money

in his family, and readily complied with his daughter's intentions. Accordingly in the twenty-fifth year of her age, while her beauty was yet in all it's height and bloom, he carried her to a neighbouring city, in order to look out a fifter-hood of nuns among whom to place his daughter. There was in this place a Father of a convent who was very much renowned for his piety and exemplary life; and as it is ufual in the Romifh church for thofe who are under any great affliction, or trouble of mind, to apply themfelves to the moft eminent Confeffors for pardon and confolation, our beautiful votary took the opportunity of confeffing herfelf to this celebrated Father.

We muft now return to Theodofius, who the very morning that the abovementioned enquiries had been made after him, arrived at a religious houfe in the city where now Conftantia refided; and defiring that fecrefy and concealment of the Fathers of the convent, which is very ufual upon any extraordinary occafion, he made himfelf one of the order, with a private vow never to enquire after Conftantia; whom he looked upon as given away to his rival, upon the day on which, according to common fame, their marriage was to have been folemnized. Having in his youth made a good progrefs in learning, that he

might

might dedicate himfelf more entirely to religion, he entered into holy orders, and in a few years became renowned for his fanctity of life, and thofe pious fentiments which he infpired into all who converfed with him. It was this holy man to whom Conftantia had determined to apply herfelf in confeffion, though neither fhe nor any other, befides the Prior of the convent, knew any thing of his name or family. The gay, the amiable Theodofius had now taken upon him the name of Father Francis, and was fo far concealed in a long beard, a fhaven head, and a religious habit, that it was impoffible to difcover the man of the world in the venerable conventual.

As he was one morning fhut up in his confeffional, Conftantia kneeling by him, opened the ftate of her foul to him ; and after having given him the hiftory of a life full of innocence, fhe burft out in tears, and entered upon that part of her ftory, in which he himfelf had fo great a fhare. My behaviour, fays fhe, has, I fear, been the death of a man who had no other fault but that of loving me too much. Heaven only knows how dear he was to me while he lived, and how bitter the remembrance of him has been to me fince his death. She here

here paufed, and lifted up her eyes that
ftreamed with tears toward the Father;
who was fo moved with the fenfe of her
forrows, that he could only command his
voice, which was broke with fighs and fobbings, fo far as to bid her proceed.  She
followed his directions, and in a flood of
tears poured out her heart before him.
The Father could not forbear weeping a-
loud, infomuch that in the agonies of his
grief the feat fhook under him.  Conftantia, who thought the good man was thus
moved by his compaffion towards her, and
by the horror of her guilt, proceeded with
the utmoft contrition to acquaint him with
that vow of virginity in which fhe was going to engage herfelf, as the proper atonement for her fins, and the only facrifice fhe
could make to the memory of Theodofius.
The Father, who, by this time, had pretty well compofed himfelf, burft out again
in tears upon hearing that name, to which
he had been fo long difufed, and upon receiving this inftance of an unparalleled fidelity from one who, he thought, had feveral years fince given herfelf up to the
poffeffion of another.  Amidft the interruptions of his forrows, feeing his penitent
overwhelmed with grief, he was only able
to bid her from time to time, be comforted—

ed—to tell her that her fins were forgiven her ——that her guilt was not fo great as fhe apprehended—that fhe fhould not fuffer herfelf to be afflicted above meafure. After which he recovered himfelf enough to give her the abfolution in form; directing her at the fame time to repair to him again the next day, that he might encourage her in the pious refolution fhe had taken, and give her fuitable exhortations for her behaviour in it. Conftantia retired, and the next morning renewed her applications. Theodofius having manned his foul with proper thoughts and reflections, exerted himfelf on this occafion in the beft manner he could, to animate his penitent in the courfe of life fhe was entering upon, and wear out of her mind thofe groundlefs fears and apprehenfions which had taken poffeffion of it; concluding, with a promife to her, that he would from time to time continue his admonitions when fhe fhould have taken upon her the holy veil. The rules of our refpective orders, fays he, will not permit that I fhould fee you, but you may affure yourfelf not only of having a place in my prayers, *but of receiving fuch frequent inftructions as I can convey to you by letters.* Go on chearfully in the glorious courfe you have undertaken, and you will

b quickly

quickly find such a peace and satisfaction in your mind, which it is not in the power of the world to give.

CONSTANTIA's heart was so elevated with the discourse of Father Francis, that the very next day she entered upon her vow. As soon as the solemnities of her reception were over, she retired, as it is usual, with the Abbess, into her own apartment.

THE Abbess had been informed the night before of all that passed between her noviciate and Father Francis, from whom she now delivered to her the following letter.

‘ As the first fruits of those joys and con-
‘ solations which you may expect from the
‘ life you are now engaged in, I must ac-
‘ quaint you that Theodosius, whose death
‘ sits so heavy upon your thoughts, is still
‘ alive ; and that the Father to whom you
‘ have confessed yourself, was once that
‘ Theodosius whom you so much lament.
‘ The love which we have had for one ano-
‘ ther, will make us more happy in its dis-
‘ appointment, than it could have done in
‘ its success. Providence has disposed of us
‘ for our advantage, though not according
‘ to our wishes. Consider your Theodo-
‘ sius still as dead, but assure yourself of
‘ one

one who will not ceafe to pray for you in.
Father

FRANCIS,

CONSTANTIA faw that the hand-writing
agreed with the contents of the letter: And
upon reflecting on the voice, the perſon, the
behaviour, and above all the extreme ſorrow of the Father during her confeſſion,
ſhe diſcovered Theodoſius in every particular. After having wept with tears of joy,
It is enough, ſays ſhe, Theodoſius is ſtill in
being; I ſhall live with comfort and die in
peace.

*The letters which the Father ſent her after-*
*wards are yet extant in the nunnery where ſhe*
*reſided; and are often read to the young reli-*
*gious to inſpire them with good reſolutions and*
*ſentiments of virtue.* It ſo happened that
after Conſtantia had lived about ten years
in the cloyſter, a violent fever broke out in
the place, which ſwept away great multitudes, and among others Theodoſius. Upon his death-bed he ſent his benediction in
a very moving manner to Conſtantia; who
at that time was herſelf ſo far gone in the
ſame fatal diſtemper, that ſhe lay delirious.
In the interval which generally precedes
death in ſickneſſes of this nature, the Ab-
beſs finding that the phyſicians had given
her

her over, told her that Theodofius was juft gone before her, and that he had fent her his benediction in his laft moments. Conftantia received it with pleafure : And now, fays fhe, if I do not afk any thing improper, let me be buried by Theodofius. My vow reaches *no farther* than the grave. What I afk is, I hope, no violation of it.— She died foon after, and was interred according to her requeft.

THEIR tombs are ftill to be feen, with a fhort latin infcription on them to the following purpofe ;

HERE lie the bodies of Father *Francis* and Sifter *Conftance.* *They were lovely in their lives, and in their deaths they were not divided.*

SUCH is the ftory of Theodofius and Conftantia, as related by Mr. Addifon ; on which I fhall only obferve that there is an interpolation in the letter written by Theodofius upon leaving his father's houfe. The paffage where he fays, ' The ftreams, ' the fields, the meadows, where we have ' fo often talked together, grow painful to ' me,' is not genuine, which indeed might be evident to thofe who had not feen the original. Such romantic trifling is not the language of a heart in pain.

T H E

# THE

# CORRESPONDENCE

## OF

## THEODOSIUS and CONSTANTIA.

# LETTER I.

### CONSTANTIA to THEODOSIUS.

IS it poffible that THEODOSIUS can approve the philofophy of *Bernier?* What would become of Chriftianity, were we to adopt the following Creed?—*L' abftinence des plaifirs me paroît un grand péché.* A fin to abftain from pleafures!—what can he mean? Is not this perfectly the reverfe of all moral and religious precepts? Are not abftinence, and mortificaticn, and felf-denial echoed in our ears from the firft dawn of reafon? Are not we taught to guard againft the prevalence of pleafures in ge-

B     neral,

neral, and to look upon them as enemies under the maſk of friendſhip? Conſider them in a religious light, and they confeſſedly alienate the heart from it's duty. The *lovers of pleaſure* cannot be *lovers of God.*—The *affections* cannot be *ſet on things above*, while they tend to earthly objects.—Conſider their moral tendency, and they will be found to vitiate and debaſe the ſoul. Selfiſhneſs, and a neglect of the ſocial duties, are inſeparable from the purſuit of pleaſures.—Theſe are jealous Gods, and demand from their votaries all the affections of the heart, all the attentions of the mind. They enſlave the better faculties, and make the ſenſes the tyrants of the underſtanding.

Surely the mind is too noble a province for ſuch rulers; and, to me, the maxim of *Bernier* appears to be no leſs inconſiſtent with ſound philoſophy, than with true religion.

After all, what I have ſaid on this ſubject is only to draw from you your opinion, which will always have great influence with

CONSTANTIA.

LET-

# LETTER II.

## THEODOSIUS to CONSTANTIA.

EVER amiable, and ever ingenious; pious in her enquiries, and modest in her conclusions;—what a pleasure is it to accompany CONSTANTIA in the researches of truth and science!—Clear in her conceptions, and acute in her expression, through the medium of her language, we discover more clearly, even those sentiments that are not unknown to us.—It assists the understanding in the same manner as the telescope aids the eye, and brings near the distant object.

THUS it is, Madam, that while you call upon me to the decision of moral or religious enquiries, and place me in the dictatorial chair; after having invested me with the commission of a judge, like a skilful advocate, you in some measure qualify me for that office, by laying before me the whole merits of the cause.

WHEN I praised the philosophy of *Bernier*, I had not indeed forgot that singular maxim of which you have taken notice; but I was by no means aware that you would seize upon this eminence, and from

thence

thence difcharge your artillery both on the philofopher and his encomiaft.

WELL—fair Friend! fince Venus is armed for the engagement, and has already made her attacks, fhe muft expect to meet with a DIOMEDE.—But THEODOSIUS, perhaps, will not be fatisfied with his conqueft; if, like her beautiful predeceffor, CONSTANTIA fhould retreat, wounded *only* in the *hand.*

YES, my amiable moralift, I do approve the philofophy of *Bernier*; nay I adopt his creed too, and cordially declare with him, *L' abftinence des plaifirs me paroît un grand péché.* What is fin? Is it not to act contrary to the will of the Supreme Being?—Beyond all doubt; where that will is known. Is it not evident that the benevolent Creator of the univerfe intended, and ftill intends, only the happinefs of his creatures?—This muft be allowed from the confent and the appearance of his works in general.—And is not *pleafure* happinefs? It muft be fo, or the term is vain. If then the Supreme Being intended *principally* the happinefs of his creatures, and if *pleafure* be happinefs; TO ABSTAIN FROM PLEASURE, IS TO FRUSTRATE THE INTENTIONS OF PROVIDENCE—to act contrary to his will; which is, confeffedly, the very effence of fin—*L' abftinence des plaifirs eft un grand péché.* It is a *capital* fin to abſtain from pleaſure, ſince it muſt have been the *primary* view of the divine beneficence, to communicate pleaſure to human nature.

To what other end was this pomp, this magnificence of beauty ſcattered over the viſible univerſe? Is not this the language of nature, through all her ſmiling works, " Children be happy—brought into exiſ- " tence by the command of that glorious " Being who is Love *itſelf,* your inheri- " tance is pleaſure, and it is your only " duty to cultivate it well." Are they not, therefore, children of diſobedence, who thus invited into the vineyard of pleaſure, ſtand idle in the market place, and vainly ſay, that *no man hath employed them ?*

Hath God created a Paradiſe, and will not man look around him to enjoy it ; but, like his firſt parent, as deſcribed by the Engliſh poet, ſtill penſively contemplate himſelf in the *murmuring* fountain ? Shall he for ever ſeek his image in the waters of adverſity ; and ſhall the fair ſcenes of life be deformed through ſuch a mirror ?

Surely to abſtain from pleaſure is no inferior degree of guilt ; ſince that very abſtinence is a reproach to the eternal and invariable Benevolence.

　　　　　　　FROM

FROM whom do we derive every appetite? By whose wisdom were the fine organs of sensation formed? To whose bounty do we owe the objects of gratification? And to whose benevolence are we indebted for the capacity of enjoyment? Proceed not these powers and faculties from the great source of all things? Was not each adapted to it's peculiar function? And is not the neglect of these capacities a fault? Is not the mortification of them a crime?

By what means came PLEASURE into the world? Was it introduced by some malignant spirit? Did some Dæmon contrive it for the destruction of mankind? That could not be; for no inferior being could have power to pervert the faculties and capacities of human nature. In such a case, the Supreme Creator must have been an imperfect being.—He must have wanted the will to secure the happiness of his creatures, or, if he had the will he must have been without the power to execute or establish it. Either of these suppositions we must not dare, nay, indeed, it would be folly to admit. Pleasure, therefore, can only owe it's origin to God, and it's very name proves it to be of divine extraction.

AND shall we refuse acquaintance with an object of heavenly descent? Shall we ungratefully bid the giver resume his gifts,

or

or reproach him with a fuppofition, that he would affect us with propenfities we ought not to indulge ?

Yes, *Bernier*, you are in the right. The renunciation of pleafure muft be a fin—not only actually, but effectually a fin. The mind that refufes admittance to fuch a gueft, muft acquire a gloomy and un-focial habit ; be fit only for the regions of monaftic dullnefs, where lazy fanctity offers a prepofterous devotion to that Being, who intended that we fhould rejoice in and partake of a general and focial happinefs.

When the bias of nature is oppofed ; when her fovereign dictates are broken, man becomes incapable of rendering any acceptable fervice either to his God, to fociety, or to himfelf ! To his God he is ungrateful, nay, he infults him with a devotion more becoming the worfhippers of *Moloch*, while he fuppofes him capable of delighting in cruelty, of afflicting his creatures, by giving them paffions, which it fhould be a merit to mortify, and of tantalizing them, by requiring a rigid abftinence from every inviting enjoyment that nature fuggefted.—To the interefts and affections of fociety he becomes cold and indifferent, when, what fhould principally engage him to them, the focial inftruments of nature groan beneath the yoke of un-

delighted.

delighted abſtinence.—Upon the ſame prin‑
ciples, he is an enemy to himſelf, to that
being which was given him for his enjoy‑
ment, and which at laſt, he ſhall render
back to the giver, with " I knew that thou
" wert an hard maſter, therefore, the ta‑
" lent that thou gaveſt me I have made
" no uſe of : Behold, here it is again."

O PLEASURE! Thou firſt, beſt gift of
eternal beneficence! Faireſt and moſt be‑
loved daughter of heaven, all hail! and
welcome to ſojourn on earth! A ſtranger
thou art to every malignant and unſocial
paſſion, formed to expand, to exhilarate,
to humanize the heart!

BUT whither has my ſubject tranſported
me? Have I loſt ſight of CONSTANTIA?
that cannot be ; for pleaſure is my ſubjeĉt.

YET, poſſibly, my amiable friend is, by
this time, more than half diſpleaſed. Where,
ſays ſhe, will this end? Has THEODOSIUS
conſpired with *Bernier* to revive the ſchool
of *Epicurus?*

BY no means, Madam! The pleaſure we
preach is not the off‑ſpring of chance, but
the child of God.

THE *Epicurean* doctrine of pleaſure is
ſelfiſh ; this that we would recommend is
pious.—From conſiderations reſpecting the
uncertainty of this life, and the improba‑
bility of another, the Athenian philoſopher,

if

if we may believe his biographer, *Laertius*, taught his followers, to purſue inceſſantly all that was called enjoyment.——From reflections that are honourable to THE ETERNAL PROVIDENCE ; that conclude him to be the liberal giver of all that deſerves the name of enjoyment, of the objects that gratify, and the faculties that enjoy - in obedience to his benevolent intentions, would we ſummon the world to the purſuit of pleaſure, and convince it that the ſun doth not ſhine in vain.

NOR will this doctrine, as my fair friend apprehends, be at all inconſiſtent with the pure precepts of that religion we profeſs.

FOR, after all, what is pleaſure ? Is it to be found at the table of riotous feſtivity ; or, in the venal arms of erratic love ? Impoſſible ! for theſe are the haunts of madneſs, of meanneſs, diſguſt and folly.

HUMAN PLEASURE is of a delicate temper. She diſclaims all connections with indecency and exceſs—She declines the ſociety of untender *Deſire*, and of *Riot* roaring in the jollity of his heart. A ſenſe of the dignity of human nature always accompanies her, and ſhe cannot admit of any thing that degrades it. *Tenderneſs, good Faith, Modeſty,* and *Delicacy* are her handmaids ; *Temperance* and *Chearfulneſs* are her boſom friends.—She is no ſtranger to the

the endearments of love; but she always consults her *handmaids* in the choice of the object: She never refuses her presence at the social board, where her *friends* are always placed on her right-hand, and on her left. During the time, she generally addresses herself to *Chearfulness*, till *Temperance* demands her attention.

LET us now, CONSTANTIA, enquire whether this amiable Being merits the charge that you have brought against her.

WILL she alienate the heart from it's duty?—But how? has it not already appeared, that she herself was sent from God, the best gift of infinite benevolence?—It is only in the abuse, in the perversion of the gift, that the heart can be alienated from it's duty.

THE lovers of pleasure may, undoubtedly, be lovers of God.—To be pleased with the gift, and not to love the giver, would be unnatural and ungrateful.—Hence the charge of the inspired writer, That some were *lovers of pleasure* more *than lovers of God*.—What was this more or less than the charge of ingratitude?

The *affections*, you say, cannot be *set on things above*, while they tend to earthly objects. Literally, they cannot;—but the best devotion, that such an imperfect creature as man is capable of paying, is derived

rived from his mortal feelings, perceptions and enjoyments.—When he finds himself happy in these, he is naturally led to adore that Being who gave them; to look up with gratitude to him, and so far to *set his affections on things above*, as he has reason to hope for a happier allotment in an improved state of existence.—Thus far, even a regard to things on earth, may assist his piety, and encourage his hope.

OUR ideas of heavenly objects are extremely abstracted from sense, and yet it is difficult through any other *medium*, to extend the affections to them.—It has been observed, with philosophical truth, by one of the sacred writers, That *if a man love not his brother whom he hath seen, how should he love God whom he hath not seen?*—I will borrow his mode of reasoning, and will add, if a man love not those gifts of God which he hath seen, how should he set his affection on those which he hath not seen?—If he hath not been pleased with those enjoyments which the divine bounty hath allotted him, as peculiarly adapted to this state of Being; what moral prospect can he have of being better satisfied in any future state?

BUT you quarrel with the *moral* tendency of *pleasure*, and load it with the heavy charge of vitiating and debasing the mind; adding,

adding, that felfifhnefs, and a neglect of the focial duties, are infeparable from the purfuit of it.—Has not my friend made a *mifnomer* here, in giving the name of *Plea-fure* to *Vice?* Change the terms only, and the charge is juft. It is impoffible that *in-nocent* pleafures fhould *vitiate*, or that *de-licate* enjoyments fhould *debafe* the mind.— It is impoffible that thofe focial delights which *foften* the heart, fhould make it *fel-fifh*, or exclude from it's feelings a regard for the happinefs of others.

IF we look into the minds and manners of men, we fhall find that not the very abftemious, the mortified, or the fancti-monious, are moft diftinguifhed for focial virtues —The reafon, I think, is obvious— when innocent appetites and defires are reftrained, the focial affections languifh under the fame oppreffion.—It is fcarcely poffible, that any man who admits of no enjoyments in himfelf, fhould be indulgent to thofe of others.—We behold innumer-able inftances of this, both in thofe who cannot and in thofe who will not enjoy.

The encouragement of pleafure, there-fore, cherifhes the focial virtues ; and he who is of a happy difpofition himfelf, will be the firft to promote the happinefs of his neighbour.

YET,

YET, will not pleafures enflave the better faculties, and make the fenfes the tyrants of the foul? No doubt—if the enjoyments of the mind are excluded; but the foul has it's peculiar pleafures which may and ought to take their turn; and if the intellectual appetites are gratified, as well as the fenfual and the focial; the province of the mind will neither be uncultivated, nor be fubject to the ufurpation of invaders.

PARDON me, Conftantia! when I write to you, I know not when to have done!—even now I lay down the pen with reluctance—even now, with a figh, I fubfcribe

THEODOSIUS.

## LETTER III.

### CONSTANTIA to THEODOSIUS.

THERE is nothing more true, than that credulity is the foible of women. I have a violent inclination to believe every word you have faid; as well your gallantry as your philofophy.—Nay, I can hardly bewail the ruin of my poor arguments, though I have the vanity to think, that the breaches you have made in them, might eafily be repaired.—However, you, certainly, had the happieft addrefs to introduce your doctrine by the hand of flattery.

The

The underſtanding of a woman, is by nothing ſo eaſily vanquiſhed, as by the artillery of praiſe.—If it be to your purpoſe to
weaken it, give it the compliment of
ſtrength. If you would blind it, call it
brighter than the day.—The praiſe of a
philoſopher is really a moſt dangerous thing,
and it is not in female fortitude to reſiſt it.
——Accompanied with the ideas of truth
and gravity, it makes it's way to the heart
without oppoſition ; and the ſenſe and dignity of the ſpeaker conſpire with our natural love of it, to give it the ſanction of
ſincerity.

Should I preclude all future compliments from the letters of Theodoſius, and
ſay no more than what is uſually ſaid upon
ſuch occaſions, *viz.* That I could not de-
ſerve them, however true it might be, it
would not ſave me from the charge of affectation—an imputation, which of all o-
thers, would be moſt dreadful to me !
Frank-hearted let me be eſteemed, and,
though deſtitute of every other excellence,
I ſhall not be the meaneſt of my ſex.

But you ſee, my friend, I have given
you ſerious, and I hope, ſatisfactory reaſons,
why you ſhould ſhut up the fountains of
adulation ; unleſs you think that they will
give fertility to a barren ſoil.—Aſſure yourſelf, I ſhall conclude this to be your opinion,,

nion, if you pay any more compliments either to my perſon, or my underſtanding.

I FIND no inclination to controvert any of the principles contained in your laſt.—— They are all amiable at leaſt, if they are not ſolid ; and, poſſibly, it may be nothing more than the prejudice of a narrow education, that would with-hold any part of the credit due to them.

AH, my friend ! for, ſurely, you are my friend, if any confidence may be repoſed in human appearances ; pity the ignorance of a hapleſs girl, I had almoſt ſaid an orphan, unaſſiſted, and uninſtructed !—Believe me, Theodoſius, to your converſation I am indebted for almoſt all the valuable ſentiments I have.——You firſt taught me to think at large.—You told me that liberty of opinion was as much a natural inheritance as perſonal liberty—that human nature had long groaned under the tyranny of cuſtom ; and that the worſt ſpecies of captivity, was the impriſonment of the mind.

EVER to be remembered is that diſtinguiſhed leſſon, which, upon our firſt acquaintance, you gave me in the Grove of Poplars. You politely pretended, that it was written by ſome other perſon for the inſtruction of ſome other lady ;—but I ſoon diſcovered in it the ſpirit and manner of

Theodoſius,

Theodofius, and found it fo well adapted to my own circumftances, that I could no longer doubt either for whom, or by whom it was written.

NOTWITHSTANDING this difcovery, I muft beg you will favour me with a copy of it; for that which you gave me has been deftroyed, I believe, by the zeal and induftry of Father M——— Adieu !

CONSTANTIA.

## LETTER IV.

### THEODOSIUS to CONSTANTIA.

BY fuppofing me to be the author of the following Letter, you have laid me under fome difagreeable circumftances; but what would you conclude fhould I, on that account, refufe you a copy of it ? Might you not juftly charge me with that affectation which you fo greatly defpife ? You fhall have it, be the confequence what it will — CONSTANTIA commands, and THEODOSIUS muft obey.

*Thoughts on the improvement of the Mind and Manners, addreffed to a young lady of Bologna : By a Member of the Academy Della Crufca.*

MADAM,

MADAM,

THE firft ftep that a young lady can take towards improvement, is to be convinced that fhe wants it.—The mind is fituated in fuch an obfcure recefs, and is fo little the object of the fenfes, that it is a difficult matter to take a view of it at all; much more to behold it in it's true light. Hence, we are apt to believe it fufficiently furnifhed, when defolate and empty; and to think it properly cultivated, though it produces little more than the rude growth of nature.

BETTER, however, is even that growth, than fome artificial products. Better is the harveft of wild fimplicity, than the rank and thriving crops that have been cultivated by the induftry of Folly!

OF all the offenfive weeds that are apt to fpring up in a young mind, and to opprefs it's better fruits, *Affectation* is the moft deftructive—where it takes root, the love of Truth and Nature perifh unavoidably, and Artifice and Infincerity ufurp their place. Qualities like thefe are fo infinitely odious, fo perfectly oppofite to all that is amiable or deferving of confidence, that, if a lady had an averfion to being beloved, fhe could not find a more effectual antidote.

NEVER, Madam, have I known an affected

fected woman possessed of any amiable, or any virtuous quality!

THE *Coccatrici* is not unknown to you. Behold in her, then, a most instructive lecture on the management of the mind! For the *Coccatrici*, with the best natural understanding, not uncultivated by books, is at pains to render herself the most odious woman in the world. *Affectation* has the absolute dominion both of her person and mind.—Her words, her motions, her actions, her opinions, are all under the influence of *Affectation*; all receive it's ugly and disgustful stamp.—Obscurely born herself, the *Coccatrici*'s passion is Quality.—Without any very striking accomplishments of person, she affects the softness, the negligence, the languishments of beauty.—These and innumerably more absurdities arising from the same principle of *Affectation*, render her the contempt of your sex, and the jest of ours.—Yet were ridiculous manners the only effect of this principle, the *Coccatrici* might be laughed at and pitied; but the same insincerity, the same deviation from truth and nature which produces these, has other consequences that render her detestable—she is scurrilous and treacherous; nor is

this

this to be wondered at. A mind which affectation has alienated from every natural principle of simplicity loses at the same time, the social virtues, and becomes indifferent to the interests and the reputation of others.

Of no simple ingredients is this character composed.—Forbidding Pride, ridiculous Vanity, insidious Insincerity, virulent Malignity, make a part of the composition of the *Coccatrici*.

Characters are always the best comments upon precepts.—In the *Coccatrici*, Madam, you behold by what odious qualities a polished understanding may be debased.

For the improvement of the manners, therefore, something more must be necessary than the mere acquisition of a knowledge; and this something I take to be the cultivation of benevolence and sincerity. An infinite number of virtues will spring from these valuable roots.—The love of humankind will make you a friend to every fellow-creature; and, together with the approbation of your own heart, general esteem and admiration will be your reward.—The love of truth will always save you from affectation, and all it's disagreeable
ble

ble confequences.—Sacrifice at the fhrine of Nature, and rather borrow from her your manners and fentiments, than from the fantaftic humours of Fafhion. From her, likewife, borrow your knowledge, and not from the labours of the fchools.—She will give you no narrow or illiberal ideas of her great author.—Be fuch writers, therefore, your ftudy, as have made her theirs; fuch as have fhewn the wifdom, the œconomy, the prudence, the benevolent purpofes of her works. The contemplation of fuch objects gives the mind a large and liberal turn; lays a foundation for the moft rational piety, and reconciles us to the allotments of life, when we behold the fuperintendence of a wife and benevolent power, over every department of the univerfe.

NEXT to natural philofophy, the hiftory of humankind will merit your attention.—Various are the advantages to be derived from this courfe of reading.—A celebrated writer of antiquity has obferved, that, he who is ignorant of what happened before his own times, is ftill a child.—Before I had made a competent acquaintance with hiftory, I never could read this paffage without pain and fhame.—I imagined that the eyes of the great Orator were upon me, and

and that I appeared childish before him. I am now extremely well convinced, that what he obferved, was comparatively juft.

IGNORANCE is the characteriftic of child-hood, and the mind that is uniformed, at whatever period of life, is ftill in a puerile ftate.

FROM the knowledge of paft events and their caufes ; from attending to the œconomy of providence in the external and internal government of the world ; by tracing the progrefs of fcience, and the gradual improvement of the mind, we learn to form juft conceptions of human actions and opinions, to make the beft ufe of reafon in forefeeing the confequences of principles yet unpractifed ; to enlarge and liberalize our religious fentiments, while we contemplate the Supreme Being in the capacity of an univerfal parent ; and to fee what moral perfection the human mind is capable of, when man in his favage, and in his civilized ftate, is diftinctly prefented to our view.

THESE, Madam, are enquiries worthy of a rational creature—worthy of that acute and penetrating genius which the liberal hand of Nature has given you !

MAKE an adequate ufe of her generous
and

and valuable gifts.—Defpife the fneer of fuperficial foppery, that is ever jealous of fuperior fenfe, and dreads the knowledge of a woman, on account of it's own igno-rance.—If you are not without hopes of being united to a man of an accomplifhed mind, qualify yourfelf for his company.— Let him not be obliged to confider his wife merely as a domeftic, ufeful in her ap-pointment; make him efteem her as a rational companion, whofe converfation may enliven the hours of folitude, and who, with a mind not vacant, or unfur-nifhed, may, like the houfeholder in the gofpel, *bring forth out of her treafure things new and old.*

To what a defpicable ftate would your fex be degraded, by thofe monopolizers of dignity and knowledge, who would debar you from both!—What! were reafon, and reflection, and memory, and every other faculty that is adapted to literary improve-ments, given to you as they are given to us, by a different author, or for different purpofes?—Mean fallacy in our fex, that would eftablifh the worft fpecies of tyranny over you, the tyranny of the mind! Groundlefs and illiberal fear in man, that he fhould lofe his dignity in the eyes of a woman, who was not inferior to him in fenfe!

fenfe! Is it the property of cultivated minds to hold cheap the accomplifhments of others? Is it not from fuch minds only, that they can meet the refpect due to their merit?—He who is afraid of marrying a woman, that is not abfolutely ignorant, gives a fair proof, at leaft, that fuch is not his own cafe.

THERE are provinces, in which our fex may properly acquire and maintain a fuperiority of knowledge, and in which it would not be worth your while to excell.— There are, likewife, certain departments in which you fhould claim, unrivalled, the compliment of excellence; but the cultivation of the mind, fhould be equally the care of both, fince nature has given to both, minds equally capable of cultivation.

IT was natural for me to digrefs, when I was pleading in favour of the privileges of your amiable fex!

To an acquaintance with natural and civil hiftory, you will do well, to join the lighter and more amufive entertainments of the *Belles Lettres.*—The ftudy of the former will enrich, that of the latter will embellifh the mind.—From works of tafte and harmony, we derive a kind of mechanical virtue, and learn to admire what

is

is truely beautiful and harmonious in moral life.—The genius of poetry has a foftening and humanizing influence on the mind; and it's pathetic powers increafe that charming fenfibility, that enthufiaftic tendernefs and delicacy of affection, which renders your lovely fex fo juftly the delight and admiration of ours.

I MEAN not, however, that by this kind of reading you fhould foften your mind, fo much as form your tafte, by admiring and attending to what is perfectly beautiful, in one of the fineft arts of imitation.

THIS art is fo naturally adapted to cultivate that harmony, which the Academics of old efteemed the effence of moral virtue, that I was always at a lofs to know why Plato would have poets banifhed his commonwealth, 'till convinced, it was becaufe they hurt the interefts of religion, and injured the dignity of the Gods, by the fportive fallies of the Mufe.

AFTER all, Madam, whatever proficiency you may have it in your power to make in literary accomplifhments, forget not that the qualities of the heart are infinitely preferable to thofe of the head. Should you be unable, for want of affiftance, or opportunity, to furnifh your mind with the treafures of antiquity; to

acquaint

acquaint yourſelf with the philoſophy of nature; or to embèlliſh your taſte by the more poliſhed labours of Genius; remember that you ſtill have it in your power to make yourſelf amiable by a ſweetneſs of diſpoſition, by an openneſs of heart, and ſimplicity of manners."

———— ————

THUS far, Conſtantia, the grave academician—you will now, I hope, not be unwilling to take up the lighter carriage of the *Friend*.——Ah! name, replete with tenderneſs!—comprehenſive of every kind, every faithful ſentiment! " Surely you " are my friend," did you ſay—Yes, Conſtantia, believe it, evermore believe it. —If every ardent wiſh for your happineſs, every active impulſe to ſerve and oblige you; if the higheſt eſteem, and the tendereſt regard, may be allowed to conſtitute the moſt eſſential part of friendſhip, *ſurely* THEODOSIUS is the friend of CONSTANTIA.

YET, too generous in your acknowledgments; too liberal even in your ideas of gratitude;—why will you attribute to me any part of your accompliſhments? Alas! what am I? The little virtues I have, if any I have, I borrow from CONSTANTIA, and by continually contemplating her per-

C                              fections,

fections, I acquire, as it were, a habit of imitating them.

CAN I make a better use of these unchearful hours, that I am doomed to pass at a distance from the friend of my heart? —*Dans ces retraites solitaires*, I find no other consolation than what writing to, or thinking of her affords me.

WHY those needless prohibitions of praise? Why should CONSTANTIA forbid her friend to compliment either her person, or her understanding?—The former has no need of, and the latter is above all compliment!

WHAT luxury in the indulgence of this growing tenderness! ah precious luxury!— perhaps, forbidden!

ADIEU! ADIEU!

THEODOSIUS.

LET.

# LETTER V.

## CONSTANTIA to THEODOSIUS.

EVER generous, and obliging; but, possibly, too tender!——Yet shall I blame my friend for his tenderness?—— Surely, no—but why " forbidden"?—— what does that mean?——shall the intercourse of friendship be forbidden?—I cannot think of that—I cannot, must not lose the friendship of THEODOSIUS.

YOU have my most grateful thanks for the Academician's letter, which I will endeavour to secure from the inquisition of Father M—. The good man has a strange aversion to every thing that tends to open the understanding.——Yet why would he keep one in the dark? Can it be of any advantage to him? In my opinion, the Academician, or, with your leave, THEODOSIUS, has incontestibly proved the female right to learning.

THIS, beyond all doubt, provoked the worthy father's zeal, whom I have heard say, That all knowledge was invested in the church.—Would to heaven, that the church would be liberal for once, and dispense a little of that knowledge to an igno-

rant

rant girl, who would be no lefs thankful for that than for it's prayers.

Will you, my friend, forgive me, when I tell you, that I have frequently wifhed you had been in holy orders, and appointed my confeffor inftead of Father M——? I flatter myfeif you would have indulged me with works of learning and imagination, and would not have confined my poor library to *Oraifons* and *Notre Peres* alone.

Pray tell me, my Philofopher, you that know the human mind, do not you think that the profeffors of religion hurt it's interefts, by purfuing them too clofely? Suppofe they fhould now and then afford us a little refpite!—Suppofe they fhould diverfify cur reading and our ftudies; fhould we not return to the attentions of religion with greater alacrity?

All thefe churchmen, however, are not equally contracted in their opinions.——I have lately ftolen the reading of a very delightful book, which, I have been informed, was written for the entertainment and inftruction of the Duke of Burgundy, by the prefent Archbifhop of Cambray, his preceptor.—I have, moreover, been told that the publication of this book was effected by the treachery of a domeftic, and that it brought frefh inconveniencies on the prelate already in difgrace!

In

In what a miſerable condition is human reaſon, when liberal ſentiments will bring a man into diſgrace! Adieu!

CONSTANTIA.

LET-

# LETTER VI.

## THEODOSIUS to CONSTANTIA.

I Rejoice that you are become acquainted with the new publication of M. *Fenelon*, the moſt amiable philoſopher that ever Europe produced! His affluence of imagination; his glowing and impaſſioned ſentiments; the attic ſweetneſs and delicacy of his ſtyle—but, above all, that delightful enthuſiaſm, which, worſhipping at the ſhrine of ſimple and beautiful nature, makes every reader a convert to her principles;—all theſe qualities give to *Fenelon* the palm of philoſophy among the moderns.

I mourn, with my generous CONSTANTIA, I mourn his diſgrace; for it is the diſgrace of my country. It is not for *Fenelon* we need repine —Reconciled to every event by the *adduciſſement* of philoſophy, is he not more happy in the confines of CAMBRAY, than he could be, if, careſſed amongſt the number of favourites, he yet breathed the unwholeſome air of a court? Zealous in the diſcharge of his paſtoral duties, a friend to human kind from principle, buſy in the exerciſe of beneficence to all orders, and all ſocieties of men—Who is ſo happy, or ſo great as *Fenelon?*

Like

Like fome fair ftar that fhoots it's evening ray
Brighter along the dim wood's opening
way,
So FENELON, by favouring courts ad-
mir'd,
More feebly fhone than FENELON re-
tir'd.

THINK not, CONSTANTIA, that I am
partial to this illuftrious man, becaufe I
have the honour and the happinefs of his
friendfhip.—The following fubftance of a
converfation, that once paffed between us,
will convince you, that I have given you
no flattering picture of him.

### Mr. De FENELON.

MY regard for you, Theodofius, makes
me wifh your happinefs; and if my longer
acquaintance with life may intitle me to
give you any advice on that fubject, I will
not be fparing of it.

### THEODOSIUS.

SIR, you will do me the greateft favour.
I have hitherto been a ftranger to mifery;
and if you would inftruct me how to preferve the happinefs I enjoy, methinks you

need

need only tell me, how I may deserve the continuance of your friendship.

### Mr. De Fenelon.

On that you may at all times rely. But our friendships, like every thing else that we enjoy, are subject to the influences of chance and time. I will give you the best proof I can of mine, therefore, while I have it in my power.————

The life of man has many cares belonging to it; but the first and greatest care ought to be that of the immortal Soul.——We cannot be too attentive to the interests of a Being that shall endure for ever, and to place any other in the scale against these, would be absolute folly.

### Theodosius

My Lord!————

### Mr. De Fenelon.

——But you cannot want convictions of this kind.——Yet there is another care of the soul which may not have occurred to you.————

Theo-

## THEODOSIUS.

I BEG to be informed of it.

## Mr. De FENELON.

HAVE not you obferved the progreffive improvement of the mental faculties, from the firft dawn of reafon, to the decline of life ?

## THEODOSIUS.

THAT improvement muft be obvious to every eye ;—but fome of thofe faculties feem to decline with life itfelf—the imagination frequently languifhes under the weight of years—the powers of reafon and reflection are, many times, almoft wholly loft ; and the memory is entirely effaced. —So far the perfection of the foul feems to depend on the perfect ftate of the body.

## Mr. De FENELON.

As the body is merely the habitation of the foul, it's tenant can no longer occupy thofe apartments that are ruinous, or decayed by time or accidents.—Hence fome of the mental faculties feem to be annihi-

lated,

lated, when they are only fufpended ; thus oftentimes we may vainly follicit the memory for an object to-day, with which it will voluntarily prefent us to-morrow. An intelligent nature cannot fuffer from material influences, and, therefore, may exift independently of them.—Nay, it may exift in the perfection of it's powers, though thofe powers, for want of their proper vehicles, are not called forth.

### THEODOSIUS.

I CONCEIVE the poffibility of this, and am now impatient to be informed, what new care it is, which has the foul for it's object.

### Mr. DE FENELON.

As the faculties of the foul are continually improveable, and cannot be deftroyed by what happens to the body, it is probable that in whatever ftate of comparative perfection they are, upon quitting this mode of being, in the fame they will pafs into another, which though higher, fhall be ftill improveable like the former.

THEO-

### Theodosius.

WHAT would you infer from hence?

### Mr. De Fenelon.

THEN, next to the exercife of virtue, the improvement of the mind ought to be our principal care: For as the former will entitle us to an improved ftate of being, fo the latter will qualify us for the enjoyment of it. From the benevolence of the Supreme Being, as well as upon the principles of reafon and philofophy, we have a right to hope that the foul, when it quits the body, will not revert to that ftate of ignorance in which it appears to be, when it firft informs it.

### Theodosius.

THIS is a very pleafing conclufion, and fuggefts to me a variety of agreeable reflections.

### Mr. De Fenelon.

I HAVE received great fatisfaction from the contemplation of it. It is pregnant
with

with many circumſtances of comfort.———
When we have been toiling for the acqui-
ſition of knowledge, we may have the pleaſure to conclude, that we have not been *labouring for the bread that periſketh ; but for
that which endureth unto eternal life.*—It muſt
be the greateſt conſolation to reflect, that
the mental improvements we make, ſhall
laſt beyond the grave ; and that the trea-
ſures of knowledge we lay up here, we ſhall
enjoy hereafter.———

IF we have contributed by our own writings to the advancement of ſcience and the
cultivation of the mind—what a glorious
reflection does it afford, that theſe effects
will laſt for ever—that the ſouls which have
received new lights, new information from
our diſcoveries, ſhall retain them in every
ſucceſſive period of being ; and that thus
we ſhall have contributed to the perfection
of glorified natures and everlaſting intelli-
gences.—There is ſomething raviſhing in
the thought—I am tranſported—I feel a
godlike pleaſure in the indulgence of it.

### THEODOSIUS.

YOU, my good Lord, who have contributed ſo greatly to the cultivation of the
human mind, have a right to all the pleaſures

sures that such reflections can afford;——
and great, indeed, and adequate to the dignity of human nature, are the objects of
complacency that attend them. But, for
my own part, I have always thought, that
every improvement the mind could make
in this state of being, would be superfluous
in another, that it's faculties would be infinitely enlarged, and that at the command
of Omnipotence, it would make a quick
transition to the angelic nature.

## Mr. De Fenelon.

For such suppositions, however common
they may be, I apprehend we have little
more or better authority than what self-
flattery will afford us: It appears, and has
ever appeared to me, more probable that
the soul should arise to a state of such perfection as we conceive of the angelic natures, by more regular gradations, than are
usually assigned to it.

*  *  *  *  *  *  *  *  *  *  *

Here our conversation was interrupted
by a letter from Madame *Guyon*; which
while the good prelate was perusing with
visible eagerness, I retired into the garden,
and

and was led into the following melancholy reflections.

" How affecting is it to obferve, that the moft enlightened minds make the neareft approaches to certain degrees of madnefs, or of weaknefs ! Genius feems to be the child of enthufiafm ; and yet enthufiafm is frequently the difgrace, the ruin of genius. The Archbifhop of Cambray, the literary ornament of Europe, diftinguifhed for the moft pure, the moft refined philofophy, is carried away by the dreams of fanaticifm, and attends to the ravings of an infane devoteé ; for fuch is this Madame *Guyon* ; and to this pitiable error of our amiable prelate, fome have imputed his difgrace."

After walking fome time alone, I was again joined by the Archbifhop, who, with that calm benignity of countenance peculiar to him, refumed the converfation. What followed would ftretch this letter too far——Expect an account of it in my next.

Adieu !

Theodosius.

Let-

# LETTER VII.

### THEODOSIUS to CONSTANTIA.

### Mr. De FENELON.

YOU will excuse me, Theodosius; a letter from Madame *Guyon* always commands my attention. That seraphic woman seems to have obtained a kind of beatification; and I look upon an address from her as it were a voice from heaven. —But I will not sollicit your attention to a subject which has given occasion to so many unhappy disputes.—I will pursue my purpose of giving you the best instructions I am able to give you, with regard to your conduct and your happiness.

BEFORE we can tread the stage of life with that gracefulness and propriety, which render every character easy and agreeable, it is absolutely necessary, that we should acquire a considerable knowledge both of mankind, and of ourselves.—This knowledge is not hastily, or easily to be obtained. —We must have mixed with society, and have attended to the different forms, that the passions and pursuits of men assume in different characters, before we can form any judgment of them that shall be generally

rally

rally adequate. I have known some men of so keen a penetration, that they have been able to judge of characters almost intuitively;—but hasty decisions, though they may often be right, may likewise many times be wrong; and they never ought to have the least weight with us in any thing, that may concern the reputation or the interest of the person we so judge of.—What I would observe, is, that there are methods of acquiring a readiness of judging; and that such an acquisition must be of great use to us in the commerce of life. —The only means I know of are those I mentioned to you—to attend to and learn the different forms that the passions assume in different characters.

### THEODOSIUS.

AND yet, my Lord, may not an artificial deportment frequently render such an enquiry vain?

### Mr. De FENELON.

IT may sometimes perplex it, but will seldom render it vain;—even artifice itself takes a colour from the passions, and they may be read and distinguished in it's operations.

THEO-

### THEODOSIUS.

. Thus you would inftruct me to know men in general ;—but may there not be a more particular procefs of enquiry, where a more particular knowledge of individuals is neceffary ? I fhould be glad to be informed how I might obtain a thorough knowledge of the man I could wifh to make my friend.

### Mr. DE FENELON.

FOR this different methods have been recommended, and different experiments have been tried. Some have had recourfe to the chymical procefs of the bottle, and others to a fictitious diftrefs ; but both to no valuable effect. The firft did not confider that a man deprived of reafon is no longer a man ; and the laft had not reflected that, on certain occafions, a man might want the power, though he wanted not the will to relieve the diftreffes of his friend.—

IF you would obtain a perfect knowledge of any man, it muft be from his domeftic character. Such a father, mafter, brother, fon, or hufband, as he fhall be found, fuch a friend will he be.—It is, moreover, in the minuter circumftances of his conduct that we are to enquire for a

man's

man's real character.—In thefe he is under the influence of his natural difpofition, and acts from himfelf—while in his more open and important actions, he may be drawn by public opinion, and many other external motives, from that bias which nature would have taken.————

WERE I once more to make choice of a friend, the firft qualities I would look for in him, fhould be *Sincerity* and *Senfibility:* For thefe are the foundation of almoft all other virtues.

### THEODOSIUS.

STOP not here, my Lord, I intreat you; but tell me how that felf-knowledge is to be acquired; the acquifition of which you have allowed to be fo effential to our happinefs.

### Mr. DE FENELON.

THERE is no ftudy fo neceffary as this; and yet, unfortunately, there is none fo difficult. Self-knowledge, like that Hefperian fruit, which was defended by the vigilance of fleeplefs dragons, is furrounded by fo many powerful guards, that it is almoft inacceffible.—Indulge me a moment, Theodofius, in my favourite province of allegory.—The moft affiduous of thefe guards is VANITY, and, at the fame time,

time, the moſt artful.—If you are determined to have acceſs, ſhe has addreſs e-
nough to impoſe upon you, and, inſtead
of *Self-knowledge*, to preſent you with a
different object, fair, indeed, and beautiful
to look upon, but very unlike the figure
you ought to have ſeen —PRIDE ſtands,
a dangerous centinel, at the gate of *Self-
knowledge* ; when you demand admittance,
he ſeats you on a throne, and bids you look
down on the crowds that ſurround you ;
you look with complacency, and return
with ignorance.—Should the arts both of
PRIDE and VANITY be ineffectual, there
is yet another redoubt to be attacked,
which is defended by SELF-DECEPTION.
This is the ſubtleſt of all the guards that
ſurround the tree of Self-knowledge—in
her hand is a waving mirrour that turns
every way, which ſo dazzles and confuſes
the ſight, that you cannot poſſibly diſtin-
guiſh the real object you aim at, from the
images reflected in her mirrour ;————at
length, with one of thoſe images you return, ſatisfied and deceived.

### THEODOSIUS.

THESE, indeed, make a formidable
guard.—How ſhall they be overcome ?

Mr.

### Mr. De Fenelon.

ONLY by the affiftance of TRUTH. As the machinations of inferior enchanters vanifh upon the appearance of an abler magician; or, rather, as the *diableries* of infernal fpirits are deftroyed by the influence of a celeftial; fo PRIDE, VANITY, and SELF-DECEPTION, fly from the approach of TRUTH.

### THEODOSIUS.

YET is it not, my Lord, a matter of difficulty, to engage this valuable auxiliary?

### Mr. De Fenelon.

—OR, rather, to perfuade ourfelves to employ him—for there the difficulty lies: —Before he can be brought over to our party, he requires fo many mortifying conceffions, that we rejeCt his fervices, becaufe we are unwilling to purchafe them at fo dear a rate.

### THEODOSIUS.

YET furely, my Lord—

### Mr. De Fenelon.

THEY are but imaginary poffeffions that he requires us to part with.—It is very true; and, for that reafon, one would think the terms not hard.—The dominions
of

of VANITY, like the gardens of *Armida*, are purely ideal, and may be given up without loss.

### THEODOSIUS.

AND yet, possibly, we are indebted to this same VANITY, for half the happiness we enjoy.—Does not the whole art of happiness consist, principally, in being well deceived?

### Mr. De FENELON.

YOU have drawn me upon a rock that I wished to avoid.—For the sake of TRUTH and VIRTUE, I am willing to persuade myself that it is not so ;—certainly, we are not deceived when we derive our happiness from the cultivation of these.—At the same time, I will own that, such is the weakness of human nature, there are a thousand *douceurs* necessary to give a relish to life, in the composition of which, deceit has a principal hand.—But what the English poet calls " The sober Certainty of waking " Bliss," that must undoubtedly flow from the exercise, or the reflection of what is real and substantial.

### THEODOSIUS.

IT should seem, then, that there are two sources of happiness ;—one from which the ima-

imagination derives fancied entertainment and unreal pleafure ; another that, arifing in confcious virtue, yields to reafon and reflection a more genuine delight.

### Mr. De FENELON.

EVIDENTLY——and we may drink at both thefe fources : But we fhould make it our care, that the fountains of imaginary pleafure contain nothing, that may tend to inebriate or diforder the mind.

### THEODOSIUS.

CAN they ever be attended with fuch confequences ?

### Mr. De FENELON.

Too frequently they are.—The imagination may be indulged, 'till it fhall acquire an habitual empire over the underftanding.—A man whofe genius and temper are naturally warm and fanciful, may give himfelf up fo entirely to the fweet influences of enthufiafm, that the powers of cool reafon and difcernment fhall be greatly invalidated, if not wholly fufpended.—

\* \* \* \* \* \* \* \* \* \*

\* \* \* \* \* \* \* \* \* \*

IMAGINE, my Conftantia, how this fpeech affected me.—At that moment the affair of Madame *Guyon* occurred to me, and

and I wept to think, that my amiable inſtructer, in his own perſon, bore teſtimony
to the truth of his obſervation.

THE remaining part of our converſation,
with my anſwer to ſome paſſages in your
laſt letter, ſhall follow this without delay.

ADIEU !

THEODOSIUS.

LET-

# LETTER VIII.

THEODOSIUS to CONSTANTIA.

"I Concealed my tears as well as poffible, while the good prelate thus proceeded.

### Mr. De FENELON.

EVERY principle acquires force and influence from habit; and if it be, as it certainly muft be, for our happinefs, to live under the dominion of *Reafon*, we fhould take care to exercife and confult it upon every occafion.———Thus it will acquire ftrength and efficacy, and our obedience to it's dictates, will become eafy from habit.

### THEODOSIUS.

THE dictates of *Reafon* are undoubtedly the laws of life.—But, in general, my Lord, how impotent and ineffectual!——What avails her legiflation, when the *Will*, the executive power, feems not to be in her intereft?

### Mr. De FENELON.

THE *Will* muft be gained over by art, and management. Where *Reafon* has not eftablifhed her empire, fhe muft do it by degrees;

degrees ;—exert her authority in little and indifferent things—make mock-fights with the enemy, and have recourse to every other gradual and persuasive method, which are made use of to reconcile us to tasks of difficulty.

### THEODOSIUS.

THIS method, indeed, my Lord, is the most promising ; but it seems that we either want skill, or inclination to apply it.— We always consider *Reason*, as imposing her dictates with a magisterial spirit.—She seems to approach us with an air of rigid honesty, rude and unpolished, as the dictator's from the plough.—

### Mr. De FENELON.

AND did the same simplicity of manners, which distinguished the age of *Cincinnatus*, prevail at this day, she would be as successful too.—Alas ! Theodosius, to the loss of that simplicity ; to our deviation from nature, we owe the greatest part of those evils whereof we complain. I think the precept most essential to the happiness of human life, is, " Live agreeably to nature."

THEO-

## THEODOSIUS.

THIS precept, my Lord, appears to want a comment.—May I have the happiness to hear the Archbishop of *Cambray* preach from such a text?

## Mr. De FENELON.

NATURE herself will here be the best commentator. She, as well as REASON, seems to have her conscience in the human mind, which fails not to reproach us with every breach of duty.

ALAS! my friend, how often do we do violence to NATURE, and cast her dictates behind! What artificial miseries do we lay up for ourselves, from the indulgence of imaginary wants!—we are not content to search for happiness within the sphere of Nature—it appears to be barren and insipid;—we fly for it into the more specious and splendid circle of Art; we are amused and dissipated in the search; but we never find the object we are in quest of.—At length, weary and disappointed, we look back to the long-forsaken walks of Nature; sorry that ever we deserted them, and ready enough to compliment them with those pleasure-yielding qualities which we should now be glad to find.—But this last hope proves frequently vain:—By be-

ing

ing long accuſtomed to an artificial life, we have loſt all taſte for ſimplicity, and what might eaſily have engaged our affections when young, we behold with averſion in the decline of life.

### THEODOSIUS.

I UNDERSTAND you, my Lord.—You would adviſe me to cultivate the love of Nature, and to plan my life upon her ſimple model, while yet I am young.

### Mr. De FENELON.

I WOULD—for the reaſons I have already mentioned ;— becauſe in her walks you will find the only genuine, the only home-felt happineſs ; which, however, you will be incapable of attaining, ſhould you defer the application, 'till the habits of artificial life have deprived you of all reliſh for natural enjoyments.

### THEODOSIUS.

THE wiſdom and experience of my venerable inſtructer would be ſufficient to convince me of the truth of theſe obſervations ; but I think I have, within the little limits of my own attention, ſeen the laſt confirmed in many inſtances.

Mr.

## Mr. De Fenelon.

It muft be obvious to every perfon who makes the leaft remarks on life, that thofe who have long lived in the circle of Vanity, can never quit it.—Not that they ftill find their account of pleafure in it; but that they are unfit for, and incapable of any other mode of enjoyment.—What veterans do we behold bufy in the purfuit of the moft contemptible trifles! What a difgrace to human reafon, to behold a countenance, furrowed with age, diftorted with chagrin over an unfuccefsful game! How difguftful to hear a matron weighed down with years, difcourfing like a girl, on the frippery of modes!—Thefe are the unavoidable effects of purfuits habitually vain.—

But when I would advife you, Theodosius, to live agreeably to nature, it is not alone that I would fave you from frivolous purfuits and fantaftic follies.—Life is not to be left unactive; and by efcaping feduction into the path of vanity, you will, of courfe, take that of wifdom. To do this, indeed, and to live agreeably to nature, are terms of almoft the fame meaning.—For the end of wifdom, is a rational and lafting happinefs, which is only to be found in acting conformably to the purpofe of our exiftence, and in treading in
thofe

thofe paths of truth and fimplicity, which nature has pointed out.

HERE my ever revered inftructer ended his welcome leffons.—I could have fpent a life in hearing him; and thereby fhould have found that happinefs, which he taught me how to obtain.

Two ends are anfwered by thus committing his precepts to writing; which I have done without much difficulty, as they are yet frefh upon my memory.—The pen is an excellent memorialift; and, while I am writing them for you, I eftablifh them more fecurely in my own mind.—At the fame time, I am convinced that CONSTANTIA will neither find them unentertaining, nor altogether ufelefs, even in her own fervice.

LET me now turn to your laft dear letter, which is not yet three days old, tho' fo much has been written fince I received it.

ALAS, my CONSTANTIA! (I addrefs you as my heart fuggefts) this delightful intercourfe may not be of any long continuance, notwithftanding your kind and tender folicitude, that our friendfhip may not be interrupted.

THE

THE fathers of Conftantia and of Theo-dofius, though their fituation in ome mea-fure draws them into a fpecious interchange of civilities, are of tempers and fentiments fo extremely different, that whenever they meet, methinks I can difcover in each, a ftifled contempt of the other. This gives me inexpreffible mortification, as I am fen-fible that this contempt in both, arifes from motives equally infignificant; the one va-luing himfelf on the fuperiority of his for-tune, the other on the advantages of his birth.

MISTAKEN men!—What are the dif-tinctions that place one man above ano-ther?—Not wealth, or titles certainly.—Genius, wifdom, and virtue alone, have this diftinguifhing power; for thefe alone are capable of enlarging and ennobling the mind, and of exalting the human capacity as high as it will go.

How long this fmothered contempt will be fuppreffed by politenefs, I tremble to think.—Upon the leaft failure of refpect in either party, it will burft into a ftorm—and—ah!—then, my fair friend!—then, farewell this dear and happy intercourfe of letters!—Farewell the delightful freedom of our morning converfations!—The fweet *fejour* at noon————

Sotto

Sotto le frefche fronde
Del frefco faggio————

and the walk at evening through breath-
ing beanfields —Ah! enchanting walks,
CONSTANTIA! when Fancy heightened by
the furrounding beauties of nature, gave to
all our difcourfe the happieft enthufiafm!

SHOULD I not tremble, even at the poffibility of lofing a happinefs like this?

—BUT let us not afflict ourfelves with
diftant evils! (O that they were far diftant!)
I'will think no longer of them, but quitting
thofe tenderly-anxious thoughts, which the
beginning of your kind letter fuggefted,
will proceed to that part of it, where you
obligingly propofe a queftion, and call upon me for an anfwer.

I AM, indeed, of opinion, that the profeffors of religion hurt it's interefts by purfuing them too clofely; particularly when
they make a merit of unnatural and un-
neceffary feverities.—Yet this unfortunate
doctrine has thrown it's galling weight on
the eafy yoke of Chriftianity, almoft ever
fince it's publication.—The fathers, thofe
fathers in whom the church has placed fuch
an implicit confidence, gave to that religion, which was meant to enlarge and humanize the mind, the meaneft and moft

'D 4                      contracted

contracted spirit and principles. — Some disgraced it by the vilest quibbles * and misquotations ; others loaded it with the most superfluous severities, forbidding the use of natural and lawful pleasures † ; —— nay one ‡ even goes so far, as to declare, that the Patriarch was deemed worthy of a heavenly vision, only because he laid his head upon the hard pillow of a stone, and what he did from necessity, advises us to do by choice.—One § has fallen into the most idle and absurd spirit of allegorizing the plainest literal narratives, facts, and precepts ; another ‖, with equal absurdity, adheres so closely to the letter, that he tells us the devil invented buskins to give God the lie, because, it is said, that a man cannot add one cubit to his stature.—In short, my friend, these lights of the church were, in general, the most miserable fanatics, ignorant, puerile, and persecuting.——No wonder, therefore, if those who consider them as guides, should tread in their steps. ——No wonder if they should cherish ignorance, folly, fanaticism, and every ridi-

---

* See Justin Martyr's ridiculous apologies for the cross.
† Athenagoras, Jerom, Cyprian, &c.
‡ Clement of Alexandria.
§ Origen.
‖ Tertullian.

culous

culous effect of blind and superstitious zeal.

Undoubtedly, my fair Reasoner, these misguided severities are ruinous to the real interest of religion ; and it's professors, as you observe, have certainly hurt those interests by pursuing them too closely.

Slavish and broken spirits may thus, indeed, be imposed upon ;—but where is that *Free-will-offering*, that rational and liberal worship, which founded in an intelligent faith and gratitude, does real honour to the deity ?—Such a worship can never be paid, 'till the mind rescued from the tyranny of an imposed belief, acquires the privilege of thinking and concluding for itself.

It would, therefore, be for the real interest of religion (if that interest may be allowed to consist in the promotion of a rational worship, and an intelligent faith) that the mind should be set at large ; and Father M——— would by no means lose his account in it with regard to your piety, though he should, as you say, give you a little respite, and suffer you to diversify your reading and your studies : For, what you observe is certainly just ; and you would not only return to the attentions of religion with greater alacrity ; but, by enlarging your moral and natural knowledge,

you

You would acquire new and nobler principles of devotion, from beholding the wifdom and benevolence of your Creator, difplayed throughout the moral and the natural world.

BUT whether or not you can obtain this
indulgence from your confeffor, you will by
all means fecure this letter from his inqui-
fitorial eye; otherwife, the fate not only
of the letter itfelf, but of the writer, may
be fomewhat dubious.

I SMILED at your wifh, that I were appointed your confeffor in the room of Father M————. If I thought you fincere
in that wifh, I fhould have very little inclination to be fatisfied; for, believe me, I
had rather ftand in any other relation to
you.—In one refpect, however, I fhould be
gratified by this appointment.—I fhould
learn the ftate of your heart; and be affured I would govern it with abfolute fway,
—that would be a circumftance worthy
my ambition.—Adieu! my amiable friend,
and remember that if ever I am honoured
with the abovementioned appointment, I
will make it my queftion, whether you
were fincere when you expreffed that wifh.

THEODOSIUS.

LET-

# LETTER IX.

## CONSTANTIA to THEODOSIUS.

I Have a thousand things to say; but where shall I begin, where end?—My heart dies within me, when I think of some passages in your last—what dreadful spirits of misfortune have you conjured up! lay them; for heaven's sake lay them again, if you have any regard for my peace or happiness—Shall I tell you that the enjoyment of your friendship is very essential to both? why should I not tell you so? Surely silence on such a subject would be a kind of disingenuity!

THIS free and candid acknowledgment, is the only return I am able to make, for all that industry of kindness I have experienced from THEODOSIUS.—Poor and inadequate is the reward, but what can I do more? Is it in my power to return those rich lessons in kind, by which I have been so much delighted,—I hope, profited?—— Exalted Moralist! amiable and excellent Philosopher! what a loss would CONSTANTIA suffer, if deprived of your friendship! To you she owes every valuable sentiment, and almost all the little knowledge she can boast;—

boaft ;—whatever, in your kindnefs, you are pleafed to diftinguifh with praife ; all, all is yours :

——Onde f' alcun bel frutto
Nafce di me ; da voi vien prima il feme.
Jo per me fon quafi un terreno afciutto,
Colta da voi ; e'l pregio è voftro in tutto.

How infinitely am I obliged to you for communicating fo minutely your converfa-tion with the excellent Fenelon ! every word of that prelate deferves to be written in letters of gold.—What fublime philofo-phy ! What enlarged morality ! What ftriking lineaments of human nature, and human manners !

But I am moft charmed with the vene-rable man, when he explains and enforces his precept of *living agreeably to nature*—I felt the truth of his obfervations without the aid of experience.—And fhall I appear vain, when I tell you, that I have always retained certain fentiments, that were of a colour with thofe of your noble friend ?— I have always thought that not only the moral but the religious happinefs of hu-man life, was beft cultivated by that fim-plicity of manners and defires, which would always attend the love and purfuit of nature. Admire with me the following paffage,

paffage, which defcribes the happinefs of the man who leads fuch a life :

E'l dubbio, e'l forfe, e'l come, e'l perché,
    rio
Nol poffon far, che non iftà fra loro ;
*E col vero e col femplice iddio lega,*
E'l ciel propitio alle fue voglie piega.

I think the fentiment in the third-quoted verfe, of uniting the idea of a GOD with *Truth* and *Simplicity* remarkably beautiful.

You fee I have already profited by the *Academician*'s letter, and have not neglect-ed the amufements of poetry and the *Belles Lettres.*—I am willing to afcribe to this ele-gant courfe of reading, ftill greater advan-tages than he has allowed it, and am of o-pinion, that the beft philofophy and morali-ty, is to be found in the works of the po-ets ; for with regard to philofophy, I would gladly be of opinion with the Englifh poet, where he fays,

How charming is divine philofophy !
Not harfh and crabbed as dull fools fup-
    pofe,
But mufical as is Apollo's lute !

I would willingly perfuade myfelf, that the beft poets are capable of inftructing us in every part of ufeful knowledge ; for I find
        a charm

a charm in their works, superior to the pleasure any other mode of writing affords me.

WHETHER it is the power of harmony, or imagination, that thus leads me captive, I am at a loss to know; whether it is the elegance of thought, the tenderness, or the gentility peculiar to poetry, that delights me most, I am unable to determine; but all together give me the most exquisite, the most refined entertainment.—I wonder not that honours, next to divine, have always been paid to poets; and that those heaven-favoured geniuses, have ever been esteemed superior to the rest of mankind. For my own part, if I should bring an offering to the shrine of any human Being, it should be to that of a poet.

ADIEU!

CONSTANTIA.

# LETTER X.

### THEODOSIUS to CONSTANTIA.

THE approbation of CONSTANTIA is more than the reward of worlds, and her favour more valuable. The utmoſt of my ambition has ever been to ſerve and oblige her, but why will ſhe aſcribe to thoſe ſervices, to thoſe poor endeavours to pleaſe, more merit than they can poſſibly have a claim to?——But it is no wonder if CONSTANTIA, who poſſeſſes every virtue in the higheſt degree, ſhould carry her gratitude to exceſs.

I WILL not anticipate thoſe evils which my fears, poſſibly too induſtrious, have ſo often brought before me ; but, while this delightful correſpondence laſts, I will ſit down, with ſecurity, to enjoy the ſweets of it.

WHAT ſpirit and ſenſibility ! What elegance of thought, in your laſt charming letter ! you have even improved upon the Archbiſhop's precept of *living agreeably to nature* ; and, in concert with the Italian poet, from whom you have quoted that paſſage, ſo juſtly admired, you have thrown a new light upon the ſubject.

NOTHING.

NOTHING could be more nobly conceived, than the fentiment of uniting the
idea of a GOD with *Truth* and *Simplicity.*—
To deify and adore thofe amiable virtues,
is certainly a very pardonable fpecies of i-
dolatry—if, indeed, it can be called idola-
try ; for we, certainly, worfhip the SU-
PREME PERFECTION, while we worfhip his
attributes, as it is only in thofe we can
form any idea of him.

AND yet it was from this fource that ido-
latry, with all it's troublefome and perni-
cious confequences, was derived of old.
When the attributes of the univerfal Being
were perfonified and exhibited by figures,
the multitude, never capable of abftracted
thinking, numbered fo many gods.

THE fentiment of your poet has, neverthelefs, great metaphorical propriety ;—
when divine honours are paid to Truth and
Simplicity, much, certainly, is done for
the fervice of virtue.

As you are profeffedly an admirer of fimple nature, I will venture to fend you a poem, which, on that account, I hope will
be recommended by the fubject.—At leaft,
I am fure, it has nothing elfe to recommend it ; and let that declaration convince
you, I have not the prefumptuous ambition,
to afpire to the name and dignity of a Poet,

or to hope that you will bring an offering
to my fhrine.

---

Written in a Cottage-garden, at a Village
in *Lorrain* ; and occafioned by a Tradi-
tion, concerning a Tree of Rofemary.

ARBUSTUM LOQUITUR.

### I.

O THOU whom *Love* and *Fancy* lead
   To wander near this woodland hill,
   If ever mufic fmooth'd thy quill,
Or pity wak'd thy gentle reed,
   Repofe beneath my humble tree,
   If thou lov'ft Simplicity.

### II.

STRANGER if thy lot has laid,
   In toilfome fcenes of bufy life ;
   Full forely may'ft thou rue the ftrife,
Of weary paffions ill-repaid,
   In a garden live like me,
   If thou lov'ft Simplicity.

### III.

FLOWERS have fprung for many a year
   O'er the village-maiden's grave,
   That, one memorial-fprig to fave,
Bore it from a fifter's bier ;
   And homeward-walking, wept o'er me
   The true tears of Simplicity.

### IV.

AND foon, her cottage-window near
   With care my flender ftem fhe plac'd ;
   And fondly thus her grief embrac'd,
And cherifh'd fad remembrance dear :
   For love fincere, and friendfhip free
   Are children of Simplicity.

### V.

WHEN paft was many a painful day,
   Slow pacing o'er the village-green,
   In white were all its maidens feen,
And bore my guardian friend away.
   Ah death ! what facrifice to thee,
   The ruins of Simplicity !

ON

## VI.

One generous fwain her heart approv'd,
 A youth, whofe fond and faithful breaſt
 With many an artlefs figh confefs'd,
In nature's language, that he lov'd.
 But ſtranger, 'tis no tale for thee,
 Unlefs thou lov'ſt Simplicity.

## VII.

He died—and foon her lip was cold,
 And foon her rofy cheek was pale ;
 The village wept to hear the tale,
When for both the flow bell toll'd————
 Beneath yon flowery turf they lie,
 The lovers of Simplicity.

## VIII.

Yet one boon have I to crave ;
 Stranger if thy pity bleed,
 Wilt thou do one tender deed,
And ſtrew my pale flowers o'er their grave ?
 So lightly lie the turf on thee,
 Becaufe thou lov'ſt Simplicity !

THERE is fuch a pleafure in the indulgence of tender melancholy and pity ;
that left I fhould deprive you of it, I will
not add one word more than

THEODOSIUS.

.* THE flowery branch of Rofemary,
that accompanies this, was gathered from
the tree, whofe genius fpoke the above
verfes.

L E T.

## LETTER XI.

### CONSTANTIA to THEODOSIUS.

YOU muſt be ſenſible that you could not oblige me more than by favouring me with any of your poetical productions.—Your Village-maid, is a pathetic picture of rural Simplicity ; as ſuch I ſhall preſerve it, together with the flowery branch of Roſemary, that accompanied it, for the ſake of the author.

YOUR laſt favour reminds me of another, which you ſome time ago promiſed, but have now, perhaps, forgot.—You praiſed the *Latin* verſes of the celebrated Engliſh poet we have ſo often admired, and called him the beſt writer in that language ſince the age of *Conſtantine.* When I complained that I was unable to read him in that language, you kindly promiſed me a tranſlation of one of his fineſt *Latin* poems, which, I think, you called a Paſtoral Elegy on the death of one of his friends, whom he expected to have embraced on his return from abroad, but found that he had taken his journey to that diſtant country,

———from

—from whofe bourn
No traveller returns———

Such a fubject is capable of great tendernefs; and, at the hands of MILTON, it
could not fail of finding it. Let me have
one more inftance of your kindnefs, in
the execution of your promife.

ADIEU !

CONSTANTIA.

LET.

## LETTER XII.

### THEODOSIUS to CONSTANTIA.

I Have made hafte to oblige you; therefore, you muft be as ready to forgive,
as I have been to obey.

The paftoral part of Milton's *Epitaphium
Damonis.*

O FOR the foft lays of HIMERIA's maids!
The ftrains that died in *Arethufa's* fhades;
Tun'd to wild forrow on her mournful fhore,
When *Daphnis, Hylas, Bion* breath'd no more!
THAME's vocal wave fhould every note prolong,
And all his villas learn the *Doric* fong.

How THYRSIS mourn'd his long-lov'd DAMON
dead;
What fighs he utter'd, and what tears he fhed——
Ye dim retreats, ye wandring fountains know;
Ye defert wilds bore witnefs to his woe:
Where oft in grief, he paft the tedious day,
Or lonely languifh'd the dull night away.

TWICE had the fields their blooming honours bore;
And *Autumn* twice refign'd his golden ftore,
Unconfcious

Unconfcious of his lofs, while THYRSIS ftaid
To woo the fweet mufe in the *Tufcan* fhade.
Crown'd with her favour, when he fought again
His flock forfaken, and his native plain ;
When to his *old* Elm's wonted fhade return'd————
Then—then he mifs'd his parted friend—and mourn'd·
   And go, he cry'd, my tender lambs, adieu !
   Your wretched mafter has no time for you.


   YET are there powers divine in earth or fky ?
Gods can they be who deftin'd thee to die ?
And fhalt thou mix with fhades of vulgar name ?
Loft thy fair honours, and forgot thy fame ?
Not he, the God whofe golden wand reftrains
The pale-ey'd people of the gloomy plains,
Of DAMON's fate fhall thus regardlefs be,
Or fuffer vulgar fhades to herd with thee.
   Then, go, he cry'd, &c.


   YET while one ftrain my trembling tongue may try,
Not unlamented, Shepherd, fhalt thou die.
Long in thefe fields thy fame fhall flourifh fair,
And DAPHNIS only greater honours fhare ;
 To DAPHNIS only purer vows be paid,
While Pan, or PALES loves the village-fhade·
If Truth or Science may furvive the grave,
Or, what is more, a poet's friendfhip fave.
   Then go, &c.


   THERE, thefe are thine : For me what hopes re-
      main ?
Save of long forrow, and of anguifh vain.

                                                    Fer

For who, ftill faithful to my fide, fhall go,
Like thee, thro' regions clad with chilling fnow ?
Like thee, the rage of fiery fummers bear,
When fades the wan flower in the burning air ?
The lurking dangers of the chafe effay,'
Or foothe with fong, and various tale the day ?
  Then go, &c.

To whom fhall I ,my hopes and fears impart ?
Or truft the *cares* and *follies* of my heart ?
Whofe gentle counfels put thofe cares to flight ?
Whofe chearful converfe cheat the tedious night ?
The focial hearth when *Autumn*'s treafures ftore,
Chill blow the winds without, and thro' the bleak elm
  roar.
  Then go, &c.

WHEN the fierce funs of fummer noons invade,
And PAN repofes in the green-wood fhade,
The fhepherds hide, the nymphs plunge down the
  deep,
And waves the hedge-row o'er the plowman's fleep.
Ah ! who fhall charm with fuch addrefs refin'd,
Such *Attic* wit, and elegance of mind ?
  Then go, &c.

ALAS! now lonely round my fields I ftray ;
And lonely feek the pafture's wonted way.
Or in fome dim vale's mournful fhade repofe——
There penfive wait the weary day's flow clofe,
While fhowers defcend, the gloomy tempeft raves,
And o'er my head the ftraggling twilight waves.
  Then go, &c.

    E       WHERE

WHERE once fair harveſt cloath'd my cultur'd plain,
Now weeds obſcene and vexing brambles reign;
The groves of myrtle, and the cluſtering vine
Delight no more; for joy no more is mine.
My flocks no longer find a maſter's care,
E'en piteous as they gaze with looks of dumb deſpair.
    Then go, &c.

THY hazel, TYT'RUS, has no charms for me;
Nor yet thy wild aſh, lov'd ALPHESIBEE.
No more ſhall Fancy weave her rural dream,
By ÆGON's willow, or Amynta's ſtream.
The trembling leaves, the fountain's cool ſerene,
The murmuring Zephyr, and the moſſy green—
Theſe ſmile unſeen, and thoſe unheeded play,
I cut my ſhrubs, and careleſs walk'd away.
    Then go, &c.

MOPSUS, who knows what fates the ſtars diſpenſe,
And ſolves the grove's wild warblings into ſenſe,
This MOPSUS mark'd————what thus thy ſpleen can
    move ?
Some baleful planet, or ſome hopeleſs love ?
The ſtar of SATURN oft annoys the ſwain,
And in the dull, cold breaſt, long holds his leaden reign.
    Then go, &c.

THE Nymphs too, piteous of their Shepherd's woe,
Came, the ſad cauſe ſolicitous to know.
Is this the port of jocund youth, they cry,
That look diſguſted, and that down-caſt eye ?
                              Gay

Gay smiles and love on that soft season wait;
* He's twice a wretch whom beauty wounds too late.
    Then go, &c.

ONE gentle tear the *British* CHLORIS gave,
CHLORIS the grace of MALDON's purple wave————
In vain————my grief no soothing words disarm,
Nor future hopes, nor present good can charm.
    Then go, &c.

THE happier flocks one social spirit moves,
The same their sports, their pastures and their loves:
Their hearts to no peculiar object tend,
None knows a favourite, or selects a friend.
So herd the various natives of the main,
And PROTEUS drives in crowds his scaly train.
The feather'd tribes too find an easier fate;
The meanest sparrow still enjoys his mate;
And when by chance, or wearing age she dies,
The transient loss a second choice supplies.

MAN, hapless man, for ever doom'd to know
The dire vexations that from discord flow,

* Milton seems to have borrowed this sentiment from
Guarini:

    Che se t'assale a la canuta etate
    Amoroso talento,
    Havrai doppio tormento,
    E di quel, che potendo non volesti,
    E di quel, che volendo no potrai.

In all the countless numbers of his kind,
Can scarcely meet with one congenial mind.
If haply found, Death wings the fatal Dart,
The tender union breaks, and breaks his heart.
　　Then go, &c.


　Ah me ! what error tempted me to go
'O'er foreign mountains and thro' *Alpine* snow ?
Too great the price to mark in TIBER's gloom
The mournful image of departed ROME !
Nay, yet immortal, could she boast again
The glories of her univerſal reign,
And all that MARO left his fields to ſee,
Too great the purchaſe, to abandon thee ?
To leave thee in a land no longer ſeen !————
: Bid mountains riſe, and oceans roll between !————
Ah ! not embrace thee !————not to ſee thee die !
Meet thy laſt looks, or cloſe thy languid eye !
Not one fond farewel with thy ſhade to ſend,
Nor bid thee think of thy ſurviving Friend !
　　Then go, &c.


　Ye *Tuſcan* Shepherds, pardon me this tear !
Dear to the Muſe, to me for ever dear !
The youth I mourn a *Tuſcan* title bore.————
See * *Lydian* LUCCA for her ſon deplore !


　　* The Tuſcans were a branch of the Pelaſgi that
migrated into Europe not many ages after the diſper-
ſion.　Some of them marched by land as far as *Lydia*,
and from thence detached a colony under the conduct
of *Tyrſenus* to Italy.
　　　　　　　　　　　　　O DAYS

O DAYS of eatacy ! when rapt I lay
Where ARNO wanders down his flowery way,————
Pluck'd the pale violet, prefs'd the velvet mead,
Or bade the myrtle's balmy fragrance bleed !————
Delighted, heard amid the rural throng
MENALCAS ftrive with LYCIDAS in fong.

OFT would my voice the mimic ftrain effay,
Nor haply all unheeded was my lay :
For, Shepherds, yet I boaft your generous meed,
The ofier bafket, and compacted reed.
FRANCINO crown'd me with a poet's fame,
And DATI * taught his beechen groves my name.

MILTON, when he was in *Italy*, had the
peculiar good fortune, to find an age of
geniufes, and to be diftinguifhed by their
favour in a very extraordinary manner.
That polifh which the young mind receives
from the elegant fimplicity of the claffics,
he enjoyed in the greateft perfection. The
confiderable fund of that kind of knowledge, which he took with him into Italy,
he had the happieft means of improving
and perfecting, in thofe infpiring fcenes,

* When Milton was in Italy, Carlo Dati was Pro-
feffor of Philofophy at Florence.————A liberal friend
to men of genius and learning, as well foreigners as his
own countrymen.————He wrote a panegyric and
fome poems on Lewis XIV. befides other tracts.

where

where the fineft writers of *Latium* firft drew their breath.————Thofe fcenes afforded the beft comment on the works of the Roman claffics, and *Milton* fhewed in all his *Latin* poems, that he tafted their beauties in the moft refined degree.

THE friend he bewails in the charming poem, of which I have made thefe humble efforts to fhew you the beauties, was the companion of his early years ; and it is no wonder that he laments him with fuch pathetic tendernefs : For friendfhips of that kind, which are nurfed under the funfhine of young enthufiafm, are always the moft vigorous.—Are they not, my CONSTANTIA ? I feel they are ; for I am, &c.

THEODOSIUS.

L E T-

# LETTER XIII.

## CONSTANTIA to THEODOSIUS.

I Flew with your letter to our favourite alcove; and there with what pleasure, with what avidity I perused it, THEODOSIUS need not be told.

I VERILY believe, that I am better pleased to be entertained than to be instructed; for I scarce ever received so much pleasure from a letter of yours, as your last afforded me—yet what can be the reason? It is not, certainly, that I am jealous of your instructive letters as giving you a superiority—I cannot charge myself with so much pride.—Nay, were I not sensible of that superiority, I must be stupid indeed ;——thus, however, I flatter myself on my penetration in being able to distinguish it, and on my modesty in being satisfied with it ; and thus, like many other good people, I am vain of being free from vanity.

BUT all the instructions of my amiable Philosopher have been seasoned with so much politeness, or conveyed in such an indirect manner, that, while I had all the opportunity of profiting by them, I could hardly ever discern that they were intend-

ed

ed for my ufe.—If then your laft letter pleafed me more than any other, it is becaufe I am idle, and voluptuous, and tafte more pleafure in poetry than in philofophy.

YET the genius of MILTON had fuch a moral turn, that he feldom wrote poetry without writing philofophy ; and even the Paftoral you have fo obligingly tranflated, is not, I find, without fcmething of it. How beautifully does he bewail the loft advantages of friendfhip !

> 'To whom fhall I my hopes and fears impart,
> Or truft the cares and follies of my heart ?

And alas ! how truly does he lament that man

> In all the countlefs numbers of his kind,
> Can fcarcely meet with one congenial mind !

Young as I am, I have felt the force of this truth, and have made many melancholy reflections upon it, after the painful, ridiculous, trifling, and impertinent vifits I have been obliged to pay and receive, from the fillier part of my fex. Horrid tyranny of faction that impofes this upon us ! What right can an equality, or a fuperiority of

fortune

fortune give one lady to rob another of her time, fenfe and patience? I fay her *Senfe*; for the converfation of fools leaves a tincture of folly upon us.——What title has drefs or figure to lay tax upon us for admiration? Do not they who expect this, infult our underftanding? And are not thofe who pay it, the flaves of folly? O that the fhackles of cuftom were once broken, and that we might chufe our fociety out of either fex without cenfure, or inconvenience!

Just before I received your letter, I was delivered from the moft defpicable and impertinent fet of vifiters, that ever difgraced the name of good company.—To me fuch vifits are always vifitations.——To the above-mentioned deliverance, you may, if you pleafe, impute fome degree of that extraordinary pleafure I afcribed to the perufal of your letter.—This I fay, left I fhould contribute to make you, what you have fo often made me, vain; and thus, at leaft, you muft acknowledge, that I outdo you in generofity.

I am not difpleafed with your obfervation, that young friendfhips are the moft tender—no doubt they are—for the friendfhips, like all other purfuits and attachments of youth, have novelty to recommend

them,

them, paffions to enliven, and enthufiafm
to cherifh them.—But ah! my friend! (for
once I will fay, my THEODOSIUS!) when
novelty is no more ; when the paffions
fubfide, and enthufiafm vanifhes like a
dream; will not the friendfhips, will not
the attachments, that thefe principles produced, vanifh with them ?—I will not fear
it, though it fhould be true.

———— ————non è prudenza
Ma follia de mortali
L' arte crudel di prefagirfi i mali.

One thing, however, I will freely acknowledge, or rather boaft of, that my friendfhip for THEODOSIUS is, exclufively, founded an efteem. For this reafon, I flatter
myfelf, that it will laft in all its prefent cordiality—why fhould it not ? It has nc-
thing to lofe, when the charm of novelty
is loft.—It's exiflence, by no means, depends upon the paffions ; it has, therefore, nothing to apprehend when they languifh, or decline.—It derives not its fupport from enthufiafm, and, confequently,
cannot fuffer, when enthufiafm dies away.

WHILE thus I comfort, I hope I do not
deceive myfelf.—But, fhould even that be
the

the cafe, let your ingenuity for once give way to your compaffion, and do not undeceive me.——This is perhaps, the only inftance in which I could be fatisfied with myfelf, for declining the report of truth.

OBSERVE, however, that I expect you will, with the utmoft candour and ingenuity, refolve fome parts of my doubts, and tell me freely, whether thofe young friendfhips which are heightened by novelty, by the paffions and enthufiafm, will not inevitably perifh with thofe fources that fupport them.

You fee I have been at pains to induce you to declare your fentiments, on this fubject; fince I have removed the principal objection, that might have occurred to you, by declaring, that my friendfhip for you cannot be affected by the argument.

ADIEU !:

CONSTANTIA.

L E T.

# LETTER XIV.

### THEODOSIUS to CONSTANTIA.

THOUGH there is nothing in which CONSTANTIA has not a right to command her friend, and though, in every thing, it is his pride and pleasure to obey her ; yet he will own, that he goes unwillingly about the task she has appointed him.——

AH! my dear, my amiable moralist ! It is frequently the happiness of man to shut his eyes against the infirmities of his nature !——In those circumstances, where the knowledge of his weakness, cannot save him from some real evil, that knowledge is of less value than ignorance.

THE benevolent purposes of Providence, have concealed the future from us, that we may not be interrupted in the enjoyment of the present ; and it is, in many cases, necessary to our happiness, that we should imitate this œconomy of the Supreme Wisdom, and embrace those innocent pleasures, which the several periods of life may afford us, without enquiring too officiously into their causes or events, and without being too solicitous about their duration.

MANY

MANY, poffibly, of our pleafures, many, I am fure, of our amufements, fpring from fuch fources, as, upon enquiry, would be found to do little honour to a creature diftinguifhed by reafon. Their tendency, at the fame time, is frequently as infignificant as their caufe, and both are unworthy of a ferious inquiry.

THERE are, indeed, enjoyments of a higher nature that may better deferve our attention ; and yet, to inquire into the probability of their duration, might contribute very little to our happinefs.———— .

SUCH, in particular, are the connections of friendfhip.—Thefe are the property of man, and muft, therefore, be frail, changeable and uncertain ,like himfelf. It muft, confequently, be for his eafe to fit down unapprehenfive to enjoy them, without meditating on all the poffible variety of evils, to which they muft be expofed, from a change of fentiments and inclinations, and from the feveral contingencies of chance and time.

IT is into the fate of young friendfhips, my CONSTANTIA, that you would lead my enquiries. Thefe, indeed, are not the leaft unworthy of our attention ; for youth is the feafon both of friendfhip and of virtue.—— If to a difpofition naturally not unfociable, we have added, the advantages of a liberal education,

education, we come into the bufinefs and fociety of life, in general, better and happier creatures than when we leave it.

We ftep into the world with liberal fentiments and benevolent affections, but the experimental knowledge of men contracts the former and ftarves the latter.—Infomuch that he muft be poffeffed of a difpofition, more than ordinarily humane, who does not in fome degree, become a mifanthropift before he dies.—I may go further, and add, that he muft have uncommon virtue and greatnefs of mind, who, with unblemifhed manners, and uncontracted fentiments, can fail with fuch a corrupted crew down the current of life.

Man is, in fpite of all his reafon, an imitative creature, and what he has been long accuftomed to obferve in others, he will, with difficulty, forbear to admit in himfelf. By habit we may bring ourfelves to behold deformity without difguft, and by being long converfant in fcenes of enmity and infincerity, the love of truth and humankind will infenfibly decay.

As youth, therefore, is the feafon of fincerity and benevolence, it muft, of confequence, be the moft promifing feafon of friendfhip; for thofe virtues are it's beft and fureft foundation.

W. **z.**

WE love a benevolent man for our own fakes, and a fincere man for the fake of his fincerity.—Efteem for ever attends the union of thefe ;—that Efteem which my CONSTANTIA has done me the honour to acknowledge, as the fource of her friendfhip!

THUS, my fair Cafuift, you fee we have a fufficient foundation whereon to erect an early friendfhip, exclufive of *Novelty*, the *Paffions* and *Enthufiafm* ; and we may juftly conclude, therefore, that fuch a friendfhip may exift, though all fuch auxiliaries fhould vanifh or decay.

YET while thefe laft, they undoubtedly yield us a more high-fet pleafure, as well in friendfhip, as in every other enjoyment.

NEVERTHELESS I know not whether much ought to be afcribed to Novelty, which, in the cup of friendfhip, is, certainly, the very worft ingredient.—Poffibly it may, for a while, give a poignancy to the tafte, but the mellowing power of Time, produces a much better and more agreeable flavour.

THE prevalence and activity of the paffions, keep up that lively zeft, and ardour of affection, which add to the readinefs of confidence, and are productive of a thoufand agreeable fenfations.

EN-

ENTHUSIASM has an effect on friendſhip proportionable to it's influence on Love.— It heightens it with the glowing ſentiments of imagination, and embelliſhes it's real advantages with the viſionary charms of Fancy, and intellectual Refinement !

YET when theſe ſhall depart with departing youth ; while *Sincerity* and *Benevolence* remain, Friendſhip ſhall remain with them.—A reflection, which affords me the higheſt conſolation ! as I am convinced that, in conſequence of thoſe principles, CONSTANTIA cannot ceaſe to be the friend of

THEODOSIUS.

L E T-

## LETTER XV.

### CONSTANTIA to THEODOSIUS.

WHAT a letter! my friend.——If you have drawn a true picture of human nature, and if the knowledge of the world, be really attended with the confequences you mention, who would not live in ignorance?—Ah! THEODOSIUS! what fears! what uneafinefs has your letter awakened!—Better, indeed, my Phifopher, had you fuffered me to continue in ignorance!—Better, and kinder, had you permitted me to enjoy my vifionary dream of the duration and improvement of human nature!—Ah! too penetrating friend!—Too ingenious in the difcovery of that weaknefs, it would have been happier to hide!—You were fenfible of this truth, and why would you gratify my impertinent curiofity, only to make me miferable?—To give me melancholy and mortifying ideas of that life in which my lot has fallen!

YET, furely, THEODOSIUS, the fweet affections of BENEVOLENCE will not wear away with youth.—If the commerce of the
world

world doth not corrupt the heart, furely, it will still have room for so delightful a guest. —I declare, that without one womanish fear, I would part with my being, rather than hold it on any other terms.

But what fuperfluous fears do I entertain? This dreadful shipwreck can only happen on the tempestuous ocean of the world—my bark, I am determined, shall not be expofed to fuch ruin.—Safely shall it steer into fome quiet harbour, and rest fecure from storms and tempests.

Seriously and plainly, my friend, you have given me fuch ideas of mixing with the world, and of the inconveniences which attend it, that I, who can boaft no fuperior fortitude, conclude, it must be my happinefs to live in folitary obfcurity.—There I can embrace your good prelate's precept, and *live agreeably to nature.*—There I shall be free from the impertinence of Folly, and the cenforioufnefs of Envy.—My precious hours will not be facrificed to triflers ; I shall employ them in ftudies worthy of a rational creature.

O Theodosius! for thofe delightful moments that shall glide away on the halcyon-wings of Peace and Tranquillity !— for thofe dear uninterrupted days of letters and leifure, when the mind may riot in intellectual

tellectual feſtivity ; and free from every low, every vulgar and debaſing care, may acquire that dignity and knowledge, which ſhall properly recommend it to ſome higher ſtate of exiſtence !

WHAT luxury is in the thought! even now I anticipate the happineſs I deſcribe. — Even now, in imagination, I enjoy thoſe eaſy pleaſures, that independence of mind and body, which ſolitude and liberty muſt afford.——I look back on THEODOSIUS buſtling in the world, pity him, pray for him, and tremble for his virtue.

ADIEU ! ADIEU!

CONSTANTIA.

L E T-

# LETTER XVI.

## THEODOSIUS TO CONSTANTIA.

"ENJOY thy dream, dear and amiable Enthusiast! Enjoy thy visionary scene! To rouze thee from those delightful reveries, to break those fancy-favoured slumbers, would be cruel, if not impious."—Such, and so expressed were my sentiments, on perusing your last dear letter.—But Tenderness must give place to Truth ;——at least in a circumstance so important, as that of laying down a plan of life.

THERE is scarce any thing in which the mind is so apt to mistake its true interest, as in projects of future happiness.—It is impossible to know how we shall bear those stations, or circumstances, which we have only contemplated at an unaffecting distance ; and yet, with an assurance that does more honour to our courage, than our discretion, we venture to conclude, that those appointments, or schemes of life to which we are perfectly strangers, would infallibly complete our felicity.

In

IN the mean time, we never confider, that new ftations, and appointments to which we have not been accuftomed, muft neceffarily take us out of our ufual train of fentiments, actions, and attentions. This, however, will make us uneafy ; for change is always an evil, and we never feel it more fenfibly, than in the manner and œconomy of life.

WITH refpect to your fcheme of living fecluded from the world, I fhould have condemned it with the fhort cenfure of a fmile, had I not paid fo much deference to your Reafon and *Judgment*, as to conclude, that thofe ought to be appealed to on every argument, that might relate to your fentiments and refolutions.

WILL my beautiful friend forgive me, then, if I fuppofe *that Judgment* to have been *bribed* by enthufiafm, when fhe concluded that, by living alone, fhe fhould *live agreeably to nature ?*

I AM fenfible, Madam, that by this you meant no more than, that fuch a mode of life would exempt you from thofe external temptations, thofe idle luxuries and follies, which are apt to make us deviate from the paths of Truth and Simplicity.——But did you confider, that to live *alone*, is to live *contrary* to nature ?————A ftate of
folitude

folitude is not the natural ftate of man.
—The arguments I fhould make ufe of to
prove this are old and obvious.——That
I may be lefs unentertaining, therefore,
while I mean to fet before you the inconveniencies attending your fcheme of life,
I will give you a fhort account of a lady
of my own family, who formed the fame
refolutions, and put them in practice.

THus her ftory is related in a manufcript,
ftill preferved among the family papers.

EUDOCIA, an only daughter, was bred
up under the aufpices of ALTHERIA, a
lady equally diftinguifhed by her piety as
a chriftian, and her affection as a parent.
The temper and genius of the daughter
were naturally warm and fufceptible ! The
offices and duties of religion had habitually infpired her with fuch a zealous and
fervent devotion, that fhe feemed to have
no happinefs, that did not flow from thofe
exercifes and attentions which religion required.

HER knowledge of books was little, of
human nature lefs. She had, notwithftanding, conceived an infinite contempt
for that world, to which fhe was utterly
a ftranger, and concluded, that to enter
into the interefts and engagements of fociety,

ciety, would be a voluntary facrifice to Vice and Folly.

EUDOCIA was in natural good fenfe, beauty, and a fweetnefs of difpofition, equalled by few women of her time.—— Thefe qualities engaged the affections of ALPHENOR, a gentlewoman whofe genius and penetration gave him a kind of intuitive knowledge of the human heart.

HE concluded, that every attempt to introduce EUDOCIA to the world, or to eftablifh the focial life in her good opinion would be vain. He knew that it would be fruitlefs to argue with her on the pleafures fhe had never known, and the miferies fhe had never experienced. —He, therefore, did not expatiate, either on the advantages of fociety, or the inconveniencies of folitude; for fuch had been the condition of EUDOCIA's life, that, as yet, fhe was, in a great meafure, a ftranger to both.

UPON the death of her parents, which happened before fhe had attained her twenty-fifth year, her fortune and manner of life were at her own difpofal.--She now determined to put in execution a fcheme which fhe had long meditated.—It was to retire, but not into a convent. A fpirit of liberty had always faved her from that facrifice, however induftrioufly folicited by the
emiffaries

emiffaries of the church, or encouraged by felfifh relations.

She was poffeffed of an eftate, fituated in a very retired part of the province of *Compeigne* ; and there it was that fhe had determined to live fequeftred from the world, with no other fociety than an aged confeffor, and neceffary domeftics.———— Of the laft fhe made a very few, and thofe females, fufficient.

At this crifis it might have been expected, that Alphenor would have ufed his utmoft addrefs to diffuade her from her purpofe.——By no means.——On the contrary, he encouraged her in her refolution, applauded the piety of her purpofe, and expatiated on the happinefs of folitary fanctity. He affumed not the leaft of the lover's character, but that of the religious friend.

By this means he gained one point, which he had ufed all his induftry, all his art to obtain.—He had Eudocia's permiffion to pay her one vifit at the end of three months after her retirement ; a favour which was allowed to none befide, either of her friends, or acquaintance, and which Alphenor himfelf, though through the mediation of religion, had fcarce addrefs fufficient to obtain.

EUDOCIA retired.—She approached the confines of her estate with raptures, and paid a kind of idolatrous worship to the venerable groves that surrounded her habitation.

" HAIL, she cried, ye innocent and hap-
" py foresters ! ye shall at once be the wit-
" nesses and the guardians of my repose.
" —Enjoy your vegetable existence, secure
" from the cruelties and the ravages of
" man !—I have fled from the evils of so-
" ciety, to enjoy peace and innocence with
" you————my undesigning friends ! my
" blameless companions ! often shall I af-
" sociate with you, and repose under the
" kind protection of your shade."

WITH the same kind of enthusiastic pleasure she walked through the several appartments of her house, consecrating each with a kind of petitionary ejaculation.

FOR the first week of her retirement, she found sufficient employment in the œconomy of her family, and the distribution of their several offices to her domestics. — The second she devoted wholly to religious exercises and the raptures of devotion.

\* \* \* \* \* \* \* \* \* \*

\* \* \* \* \* \* \* \* \* \*

F          I HAVE

I HAVE been interrupted, and you will not at prefent, be troubled with any further account of my pious anceftor.

ADIEU !

THEODOSIUS.

# LETTER XVII.

## THEODOSIUS to CONSTANTIA.

\* \* \* *BUT* whatever is rapturous cannot laſt long : Thoſe exerciſes that lift the mind above it's uſual pitch, if too frequently, or too long indulged, will at length, either totally deſtroy it, or deprive it of that ſobriety, which is neceſſary for the preſervation of it's due poiſe.

NATURE ſeems, in kindneſs, to have guarded us againſt the inconveniences that might ariſe from hence, by ſhortening the influence of joy, by inclining us to variety, and by giving the property, either of indifference, or diſguſt to every object, that has been too long, or too aſſiduouſly purſued, with whatever avidity it might have been embraced at firſt.

THAT little ſociety to which EUDOCIA had hitherto been accuſtomed, was a neceſſary relief from the aſſiduities of religious ſtudies and exerciſes ; and, far from being any prejudice, was in reality, favourable to the intereſts of religion.—It is certain, however, that ſhe was of a different opinion, upon her firſt ſecluſion from the world ; but many weeks had not paſſed,

before

before she felt the inconveniencies of her mistake, if she was unwilling to perceive the mistake itself.

THE exercises of devotion, by being too frequently repeated, became languid and unaffecting : Her mind, having been accustomed to communication, shrunk under the weight of it's own sentiments ; and every succeeding day approached less welcome, and more feared than the former.

WHAT should she do ? Should she return to that world she had forsaken and despised ? But, a sense of shame and pride rose in opposition to that thought, and strangled it in it's birth.

IN this dissatisfied and dejected state, she recollected the appointment of ALPHENOR'S visit—with joy she recollected it, and remembered, with a blush, the difficulties she had started against it.

" How, said she, shall I conceal that
" pleasure, which I cannot but feel at the
" sight of ALPHENOR ? If I express my real
" sentiments, he will have reason to think
" his presence of some consequence to my
" happiness ; and if I receive his visit with
" an indifference equal to that with which
" I received the proposal of it, I shall do
" violence to that candour and sincerity of
" heart, which cannot bear even the sha-
" dow

" dow of diffimulation.——In the former
" cafe, I fhould appear a weak and un-
" fteady creature to ALPHENOR.—In the
" latter, I fhould become infupportable to
" myfelf."

WHILE fhe was thus meditating, in
what manner fhe fhould receive her friend,
the time appointed for his vifit was at hand.
—But ALPHENOR did not appear—mafter
of every key to the human heart, he knew
that if, by delaying his vifit to EUDOCIA,
he gave it the appearance of uncertainty,
that uncertainty would probably create an
anxiety on her part, which might not be
unfavourable to his defign.

THIS had the defired effect : Day after
day paffed away in the fame folitary languor, and EUDOCIA concluded, that the
many objections fhe had made to ALPHENOR's vifit, had determined him at laft, to
think of it no more.—This reflection made
her miferable, and fhe now wifhed for nothing fo ardently, as that the prefence of
her friend would prove thofe apprehenfions
vain.

AT length he came.—A tear fell from
the eye of EUDOCIA, when fhe received
him ; he obferved it, and knew that he had
now nothing more to do, than to reconcile
her to herfelf, and to enable her to acknow-

ledge

ledge her mistake without shame, or confusion.

THOSE wants that invention or eloquence could supply never distressed him long.

"I HOPE, Madam;" said he, "that a
"life of solitude has been more comfort-
"able to you than it has been to me."—
"How," cried EUDOCIA, "has ALPHENOR
"been a Solitaire?"

"Such, Madam, I have been ever since
"I lost the happiness of EUDOCIA's con-
"versation.—It was always my ambition
"to imitate her,—Shall she, said I, shall a
"woman have fortitude to forsake the
"world, and retire to solitude, to practise
"the sublime duties of religion; and shall
"I not profit by the example of that virtue
"I cannot but praise?—But alas! Madam!
"alas! EUDOCIA! shall I confess to you—"

"WHAT would ALPHENOR confess?
"Either the miseries and the inconveni-
"ences of absolute solitude must be very
"great, or I must have an uncommon
"and disgraceful weakness of mind; for
"the time I have thus devoted, I have not
"spent in happiness, but in languor and
"discontent."

EUDOCIA shed another tear.

"How kind, said ALPHENOR, thus to
"pity the unhappiness of your friend!"

I CAN-

" I CANNOT, replied EUDOCIA, accept
" of a compliment I do not deferve. The
" tear you obferved had fomething felfifh
" in it.—ALPHENOR can have no weak-
" nefs, that is not the weaknefs of human
" nature; and, could it be any fatisfaction
" to him to know, that his friend has been
" as miferable in a ftate of folitude as him-
" felf, his own ingenuous confeffion might
" countenance her in acknowledging it."

FOR a woman of my CONSTANTIA's penetration, it would be needlefs to tranfcribe
any more of the above narrative; and it
will be fufficient to inform her, that from
the union of ALPHENOR and EUDOCIA, in
a diftant defcent, came

THEODOSIUS.

LET.

# LETTER XVIII.

## CONSTANTIA to THEODOSIUS.

OH! Theodofius!—my guide—my friend!—my inftructer! alas!—no more!———

THE tear fwims in my eye—my heart fwells; and my hand trembles while I tell you, that you are—banifhed for ever from this place, and that I am forbidden to fee you, or hear from you more.

WHAT, what fhall I do? nothing ever can repair this cruel lofs—the lofs of a wife, a learned, and a virtuous friend! What has the world of equal worth?—Deprived, for ever deprived of that prefence, which enlivened with invariable chearfulnefs and fenfibility!—of that converfation which never failed to make the mind richer, the heart happier—and (O cruel extenfion of refentment!) of that precious, that inftructive correfpondence, which, as it afforded me the beft means of cultivating and improving my mind, ought to have been confidered with gratitude by the very perfon who has forbidden it.

BUT of whom, or of what do I prefume to complain? Duty reftrains the remon-
ftrances.

ftrances of grief, and the expoftulations of forrow.—You are not now ignorant, that the quarrel you dreaded, has actually hap-pened, with the bittereft recriminations.

THEN, farewell, my beft, and moft va-luable friend !—for ever to be remember-ed !—for ever to be regretted !—Accept of all I can return for your invariable, your induftrious kindnefs !—Moft refpected of men !—moft efteemed of friends !—Ac-cept the gratitude of a tear, and think of

CONSTANTIA.

L E T.

# LETTER XIX.

## To THEODOSIUS.

## From an unknown Hand.

THE writer of this letter is not a ſtranger to the mutual regard of THEODOSIUS and CONSTANTIA.—From ſure authority he knows, that the hand of that lady is, by the appointment of her father, in which, it. ſeems, ſhe has acquieſced, within two days to be given to another. THEODOSIUS will make what uſe he thinks proper of this information, and conclude that he receives it from

A FRIEND.

LET-

# LETTER XX*.

### THEODOSIUS to CONSTANTIA.

THE thought of my CONSTANTIA, which has for some time been my only happiness, is now become a greater torment to me than I am able to bear.— Must I then live to see you another's ?— Death is in the thought ; and, indeed, life itself is now become a burthen to me.— May you long be happy in the world, but forget that there was ever such a man in it as

THEODOSIUS.

* This letter, which, with some little variations, is recorded by the Spectator, No. 164, concludes the Correspondence of THEODOSIUS and CONSTANTIA, from their first acquaintance to the departure of THEODOSIUS.

# THE END.

Lightning Source UK Ltd.
Milton Keynes UK
UKHW022303291118
333191UK00011B/915/P